Associations in Action:
The Washington, D.C., Higher Education Community

by Harland G. Bloland

ASHE-ERIC Higher Education Report No. 2, 1985

Prepared by

 ® *Clearinghouse on Higher Education*
The George Washington University

Published by

Association for the Study of Higher Education

Jonathan D. Fife,
Series Editor

Cite as:
Bloland, Harland G. *Associations in Action: The Washington,
D.C., Higher Education Community*. ASHE-ERIC Higher Edu-
cation Report No. 2. Washington, D.C.: Association for the
Study of Higher Education, 1985.

The ERIC Clearinghouse on Higher Education invites individuals
to submit proposals for writing monographs for the Higher
Education Report series. Proposals must include:
1. A detailed manuscript proposal of not more than five pages.
2. A 75-word summary to be used by several review committees
   for the initial screening and rating of each proposal.
3. A vita.
4. A writing sample.

Library of Congress Catalog Card Number: 85-72833
ISSN 0884-0040
ISBN 0-913317-21-7

ERIC® **Clearinghouse on Higher Education**
The George Washington University
One Dupont Circle, Suite 630
Washington, D.C. 20036

ASHE **Association for the Study of Higher Education**
One Dupont Circle, Suite 630
Washington, D.C. 20036

This publication was partially prepared with funding from the
National Institute of Education, U.S. Department of Education
under contract no. 400-82-0011. The opinions expressed in this
report do not necessarily reflect the positions or policies of NIE
or the Department.

EXECUTIVE SUMMARY

What Are Higher Education Associations, and Who Needs Them?

In the United States, associations are organizations in which membership is voluntary. They have been positively viewed as integrators of society (Rose 1955; Smelser 1963), as socially stabilizing forces (Coser 1956; Lipset 1960), and as vehicles for the direct expression of public opinion (Commager 1947). Less positively, they have been seen as lobbyists for special interests, undemocratic veto groups, and groups with too much power in relation to political parties and elected public officials (McConnell 1966). All of these perspectives, except the last, have been applied to higher education associations. They have never been viewed as being as powerful in relation to public officials as, say, interest groups representing business, labor, agriculture, or the professions.

Colleges and universities are the institutional members of the associations described in this monograph. They join Washington-based higher education associations because they need to have the case for higher education presented to Congress and to the administration. They need constant, skillful monitoring of federal government decisions, and they need to be kept abreast of the shifting winds of policy making. Institutions of higher education require that their autonomy be protected from excessive federal regulation. They not only must have representation for the whole enterprise of higher education, but they also join specific associations because those associations speak for particular sectors of education. The associations provide services to colleges and universities—leadership programs, important forums, and research results.

How Has the Higher Education Community in Washington Developed, and How Has It Fared?

The associations in Washington entered the 1960s with a "traditional perspective" regarding their political role. Their activities reflected the notions that higher education was a good in itself and would therefore have society's unquestioned support, that higher education need only fulfill its traditional missions of teaching, research, and community service as the institutions defined them to be supported, and that these missions were so important that higher education should be protected from governmental interference as it pursued its lofty aims (King 1975, pp.68–70).

The organization of associations in Washington and the methods of operation that grew from this perspective tended to give higher education a small, rarely influential voice in federal education policy. The Washington offices of the associations were quite small and in many cases directed by amateurs more familiar with campus life than with the rough-and-tumble politics of Washington. The process of influencing and responding to legislation and decisions of importance to higher education suffered in at least three ways. First, the associations tried to avoid even the appearance of lobbying, so they were passive and diffident about articulating the interests and needs of higher education. Second, when called upon to express their views on pending legislation, associations referred questions to their membership's leaders, the college and university presidents. They, in turn, debated the pros and cons of the issue, sometimes for a considerable length of time, before replying. This process was so cumbersome that decisions affecting higher education were made while association members were still discussing matters, and higher education had no impact on the decision (Babbidge and Rosenzweig 1962). Third, when presidents of colleges and universities did discuss important issues, they invariably did not confine themselves to stating their requirements and recommending the best ways to fulfill them. Instead, they took up the broad questions of public policy and in high-minded discussions seemed ready to advise Congress on how to solve, for example, the church/state problem (Babbidge and Rosenzweig 1962, p. 111).

The 1960s was a transition period in which the associations moved from a traditional perspective to ''pragmatic realism'' (King 1975); thus, while the associations wanted to retain much of the traditional perspective, the overwhelming consequence of the major higher education legislation of that period was that associations had to become more politically active or be bypassed and superseded by other forms of representation. The long-time coordinating function of the American Council on Education, for example, was reemphasized and federal relations given a more significant role in the association's total activities. Mechanisms for cooperation among associations came into being (the Secretariat, the Morse Federal Relations Group, for example), and norms (principles by which the associations tried to order their relationships) emerged in the 1960s. These events indicated that the Washington higher education associations were evolving into a true community, trying to act on the beliefs that associations should deemphasize disagreement, consult with each other, seek unity wherever possible, and emphasize areas of agreement.

By the early 1970s, the associations had organized a fairly effective community for making their views known in Washington, and they were often successful in presenting a united perspective to Congress when asked to present views on pending legislation. One such basis for unity was the communitywide conviction that the next positive step in higher education programs was for the federal government to provide support for higher education through substantial direct grants to institutions in the 1972 Amendments to the Higher Education Act of 1965. In this stance, however, the associations and their institutional members were almost alone, as most of Congress, a major proportion of the interested publics, and the administration favored direct aid to students. When the smoke and dust of that legislative struggle had cleared and it was evident that the thrust of federal support was to be student aid, the associations were viewed as having been out of touch. Although this negative opinion clung to the associations through much of the 1970s, it bore little relation to reality. Out of the ashes of the 1972 disaster, the associations forged a revitalized community: Associations upgraded their federal relations activities, recruited staff with experience and expertise in Washington, became proactive rather than reactive in anticipating and dealing with federal decisions and legislation, vastly improved communication among the associations and with the federal government, and generally and specifically increased their willingness and capacity to interact with the federal government. Of course, many other factors in addition to the events surrounding the 1972 Amendments galvanized the associations (the new depression in higher education, the ever-growing regulatory presence of the government). But the 1972 Amendments marked a time and an event that indicated a transition from the fading traditional orientation of the 1960s to the pragmatic realism and political activism of the 1970s and 1980s.

By the end of the 1970s, the associations had successfully participated in the 1976 Amendments, the Middle Income Assistance Act of 1978, and the 1980 Amendments to the Higher Education Act. In this process, they had temporarily resolved some deep-seated differences between public and private institutions.

The election of Ronald Reagan to the presidency ushered in a new and, for a time, bewildering political environment for higher education in Washington. Not only did the new administration advocate dismantling the fledgling Department of Education, but almost all domestic programs, including higher education, were scheduled for substantial cutbacks or termination. In addition, old friends of higher education were no longer in Congress, and the "liberal consensus," which strongly supported aid to higher education, seemed to be disintegrating (Finn 1980). For the associations, the 1980s have been a period of fine tuning the mechanisms already in place that bring service and give voice to higher education in Washington. Perhaps most important, the associations have been crucial in keeping the structure of higher education support intact in the face of proposed Draconian cuts in federal financial support to higher education. The associations, through their Action Committee for Higher Education, organized an effective grass roots campaign urging parents, students, higher education officials, and others to protest the cuts in federal aid. The speed and skill with which the campaign was organized and implemented indicated both the effectiveness of the higher education community's organizational machinery and the new realization that the mobilization of a broader constituency would be part of the future activities of the community.

As the second half of the 1980s approaches, the associations in Washington can look back upon two solid areas of achievement. They have been influential in shaping and protecting federal support for higher education, and they have perfected organizational and communitywide mechanisms for effectively serving their constituents. Of course, they have not solved all the problems, nor are they central players in the Washington political arena. They are faced in the mid-1980s with an approaching crisis that threatens the unity and effectiveness of the community. The current student aid legislation, as its benefits are eroded by insufficient funding and inflation, strikes the private sector as deeply threatening to the economic health of independent institutions. At the same time, it forcefully communicates to the public sector that it appears to have given away too much in the negotiations for the 1980 Amendments. Public institutions believe that equal opportunity for minorities and the poor is in danger. The private and public sectors have already clashed sharply on this issue, and it may be that an entirely new legislative basis for federal support to higher education needs to be constructed when the current legislation expires in 1985.

ADVISORY BOARD

Roger Baldwin
Assistant Professor of Education
College of William and Mary

Robert Birnbaum
Professor of Higher Education
Teachers College, Columbia University

Susan W. Cameron
Assistant Professor and Chair
Higher/Postsecondary Education
Syracuse University

Clifton F. Conrad
Professor of Higher Education
University of Arizona

George D. Kuh
Associate Dean for Academic Affairs
School of Education
Indiana University

Yvonna S. Lincoln
Associate Professor of Higher Education
The University of Kansas

Robert A. Scott
President
Ramapo College of New Jersey

CONSULTING EDITORS

Robert Atwell
President
American Council on Education

Robert Cope
Professor of Higher Education
University of Washington

Robert L. Craig
Former Vice President, Government Affairs
American Society for Training and Development, Inc.

John W. Creswell
Associate Professor
Department of Educational Administration
University of Nebraska

David Kaser
Professor
School of Library and Information Science
Indiana University

George Keller
Senior Vice President
Barton-Gillet Company

David W. Leslie
Professor and Chair
Department of Educational Leadership
The Florida State University

Linda Koch Lorimer
Associate General Counsel
Yale University

Ernest A. Lynton
Commonwealth Professor and Senior Associate
Center for the Study of Policy and the Public Interest
University of Massachusetts

Gerald W. McLaughlin
Institutional Research and Planning Analysis
Virginia Polytechnic Institute and State University

Theodore J. Marchese
Vice President
American Association for Higher Education

Virginia B. Nordby
Director
Affirmative Action Programs
University of Michigan

Harold Orlans
Office of Programs and Policy
United States Civil Rights Commission

Lois S. Peters
Center for Science and Technology Policy
New York University

John M. Peterson
Director, Technology Planning
The B. F. Goodrich Company

Marianne Phelps
Assistant Provost for Affirmative Action
The George Washington University

Richard H. Quay
Social Science Librarian
Miami University

Charles B. Saunders, Jr.
Vice President for Government Relations
American Council on Education

John E. Stecklein
Professor of Educational Psychology
University of Minnesota

Donald Williams
Professor of Higher Education
University of Washington

CONTENTS

Foreword	**xv**
Introduction	**xix**
Higher Education Associations and Society	**1**
The Formation of Associations	5
Association Membership: Why Members Join and Why They Stay or Exit	7
The Washington-Based Education Association Community and Its Environment	**13**
Demystifying Variety and Fragmentation: Classification Schemes	13
Zeroing In on the Big Six (or Seven)	14
The Satellites	22
The Policy Arena	24
In the Shadow of Elementary and Secondary Education: Higher Education and the Federal Government	28
Three Political Perspectives	33
The 1960s: Steps toward a Cooperating Community	**37**
The Associations' Response	38
The Creation of Community: Cooperative Mechanisms and Community Norms	39
Community Norms	41
The Close of the Decade	42
The 1970s: The Nixon-Ford-Carter Years	**49**
The Quest for Unity and the 1972 Higher Education Amendments	49
Government Regulations and Student Aid	51
The Distribution of Federal Funds and Institutional Problems	53
The Haves and the Have Nots	54
The Washington Education Associations Engage the 1970s	56
Community Changes and Activities	62
The Improving Image: The Big Six in the 1970s	67
Tax Credits and the Middle Income Student Assistance Act of 1978	70
The Department of Education	71
The Higher Education Reauthorization Act of 1980	72
End of the 1970s: Internal Turmoil and Solving Problems	74

The 1980s: Confronting the Reagan Administration 79
The National Elections of 1980 and Their Aftermath 79
The Reagan Presidency 80
The Associations and the Reagan Budget for 1983 81

Current Issues and the Future: The Washington Community in the Last Half of the Decade 83
The Present Environment 83
What Lies Ahead? 88

References 91

Index 99

FOREWORD

For us here at the Association for the Study of Higher Education and the ERIC Clearinghouse on Higher Education, this report represents a different type of monograph. The ASHE-ERIC Higher Education Report series is designed to analyze conventional wisdom—research, literature, and institutional experiences—so administrators and scholars can apply the sum total to their own situations. While including the literature survey and issue analysis that have become series trademarks, this book differs from our usual reports in that it is partly original research and partly literature survey. Harland Bloland contributes research, updating the information available on the subject done by Stephen Bailey (1975), Lauriston King (1975), and Lawrence Gladieux with Thomas Wolanin (1976).

Sooner or later, every individual and every institution recognizes that effective policy on a national level, be it legislative, regulatory, or research-oriented, requires unified action and coordinated effort. The national higher education community is no exception. Over the years, various associations have joined other members of the community to protect their interests, advance their causes, and enable them to operate more effectively. The associations covered by this report are those that are located in Washington, D.C.. Each association's national headquarters serves many functions for its members: stimulating communication, conducting annual meetings, holding workshops, publishing reports, and alerting them to federal and state legislation affecting higher education. The direct influencing of this legislation, or lobbying, has been considered in the past as vulgar, distasteful, and beneath academic dignity. In reality, lobbying actually means letting the people in legislative decision-making positions know the needs and positions of the higher education community. Furthermore, associations act as a counterweight to the pervasive influence of non-higher education interest groups, which by necessity are competing for the same monies.

Dr. Bloland, professor of higher education at the University of Miami, has long had an interest, both as scholar and practitioner, in the role of associations on higher education. In practice, he is organization advisor for the State and Regional Research Associations Special Interest Group of the American Educational Research Association. As a scholar, he is known for his writing on associations,

---

particularly the *Report on the Higher Education Secretariat Community* in 1971. For Dr. Bloland, this report constitutes more than fifteen years of study and observations.

Whether providing institutional consensus before a Senate subcommittee hearing, defending rights of members in a bargaining session with a university, or arranging a conference to bring members together, the higher education associations have long proved their worth to their thousands of constituents. Yet the next few years may be perhaps the most crucial in terms of defining the role of the federal government in higher education since the 1960s. For the foreseeable future, institutional funding and policy making will be intertwined with federal and state budgeting and policies. To have any voice in this important process, the higher education community must maintain and expand its contacts in the legislative process. The higher education community has earned its rightful place in the appropriations process, but only diligent action will ensure that higher education continues to receive equitable attention.

Jonathan D. Fife
Series Editor
Professor and Director
ERIC Clearinghouse on Higher Education
The George Washington University

ACKNOWLEDGEMENTS

I want to thank the people in the associations for the time they have spent with me. Also let me thank the chief executive officers of the higher education community for their cooperation.

INTRODUCTION

Although a great many associations represent postsecondary education, for the past 25 years seven associations headquartered in Washington, D.C., have been particularly active and visible in giving voice to the interests of postsecondary education as a whole and representing the most prominent institutional sectors of higher education in the United States (public and private institutions, graduate and research universities, liberal arts colleges, and community colleges). These seven associations—the American Council on Education, the National Association of State Universities and Land-Grant Colleges, the American Association of State Colleges and Universities, the American Association of Community and Junior Colleges, the Association of American Universities, the Association of American Colleges, and the National Association of Independent Colleges and Universities—cover the widest and most comprehensive range of national issues that concern higher education. (At any one time, the community has been comprised of the "Big Six" associations. The Association of American Colleges represented the independent sector until 1976, and the National Association of Independent Colleges and Universities became chief representative for that sector in 1976.)

Based on a belief that academic institutions must be apart from the political arena to retain their autonomy and because higher education was associated with the objective pursuit of knowledge and not dedicated to the pursuit of its own self-interest, higher education until the 1960s took the position that it should be above politics and policy making. But times changed and national needs required higher education to supply skilled and highly educated graduates for the work force. It accomplished this task in part through a vast array of federal grants, contracts, and aid legislation. This government activity "served as a magnet to draw distant association headquarters like iron filings to the field of force of the nation's capital" (Bailey 1975, p. iv).

Although still reluctant, higher education associations and their leaders were pulled into ever more complicated and demanding relationships with the federal government, with each other, and with their members. This report traces the development of the role of higher education associations in Washington from the 1960s to the present, describing and analyzing the events, problems, and issues associated with them. It defines voluntary associations and indicates why members join, remain, and/or leave; explains the various classification schemes that have been used to make sense of the bewilderingly large number and types of national associations, focusing on the Big Six national higher education associations; describes the policy-making arena for higher education and the general principles that guide federal higher education decision making and three political perspectives that have oriented Washington representatives in their thinking about the role of associations in national affairs; and tracks the changing role of the associations as they deal with the shifting national political scene.

Although they are enmeshed in almost every issue, important event, and educational crisis that higher education must confront, Washington higher education associations are an understudied element of higher education. One consequence is that this monograph, particularly for sections covering the late 1970s and 1980s, relies upon such everyday sources as the *Chronicle of Higher Education, Change* Magazine, ACE's *Higher Education and National Affairs,* newspaper accounts, association annual reports, and conversations with association leaders. A well-developed, up-to-date, theoretically sophisticated research literature on the late 1970s and 1980s does not exist, and it is the author's hope that this monograph will lay the foundation for more extensive research and study.[1]

1. A small number of superb studies cover the 1960s and 1970s, however; see, for example, Babbidge and Rosenzweig 1962, Finn 1978, Gladieux and Wolanin 1976, King 1975, and Pettit 1965.

HIGHER EDUCATION ASSOCIATIONS AND SOCIETY

Higher education associations belong to a category of organizations called "voluntary associations"; they are groups of persons organized to pursue interests common to their members. Membership is neither mandatory nor assumed by birth, and the groups are organized separately from the state, although in many instances government bureaus and departments organize associations to fulfill an agency's goals (Sills 1968, p. 363).

Members of higher education associations might be individuals, institutions, or other associations. Individual members frequently are part-time, nonsalaried, voluntary participants in the association's affairs, whereas in the colleges and universities they represent, they are full-time, salaried staff members. Most national higher education associations have a central, full-time, salaried administrative staff.

The voluntary association has been viewed as a "tangential" organization:

> *It is a group in continuing patterns of interaction that functions as a "bridge" between persons in two or more institutionalized groups or subdivisions thereof. The word "tangent" is appropriate because it suggests a set of relationships that are in a sense peripheral to that defining the central functions of the institutionalized groups* (Truman 1955, pp. 40–41).

Thus, for example, the relationships among professors that constitute the basis for organizing a learned society are tangential to the professor/student/administrator relationships central to the research/teaching functions of a university.

The distinction between university and association is actually more ambiguous, because associations, particularly in recent years, have engaged in myriad teaching activities. They sponsor workshops, institutes, and short courses year round, and they engage directly and often competitively in seeking funds for and in conducting research studies. Nevertheless, the distinction is useful, and in this report associations are viewed essentially as "tangential" to the "basic organizational units," universities and colleges.

Most general studies of voluntary associations where the emphasis is on the community voluntary associations have focused on determining how the associations relate to the social and political order. They have been viewed, for example, as a basic means for integrating the society (Babchuck and Warriner 1965; Rose 1955; Smelser 1963). Some have extolled the virtues of multiple, crosscutting, or overlapping memberships in associations as major sources of restraint, stability, and cohesion in democratic systems (Coser 1956; Lipset 1960). Others have viewed associations as purveyors of conservative bias in pluralist societies (McConnell 1966; Schattschneider 1960).

The most compelling broad concern regarding voluntary associations has been their role in building and maintaining political democracy. Voluntary associations, for example, are seen as significant buffers, mediating between the overwhelming power of the state and the weakness and vulnerability of the individual (Nall 1967, p. 279). One especially lively controversy in this area has turned on the question of whether or not the governing structures of associations must themselves be democratic for the larger system to sustain democracy (Lipset, Trow, and Coleman 1962; Michels 1915).

De Tocqueville, whose name tends to come up in discussions of associations, saw them as the primary means for the creation of a democratic expression of public opinion (Commager 1947, p. 279). Associations, in the literature on organized interest groups (particularly pressure groups and lobbies), are viewed as providing far greater leverage in the pursuit of interests than would be possible through individual or unorganized group action (Hrebener and Scott 1982; Moe 1980; Wilson 1981).

The literature that stresses the relationship of associations to democracy is not all optimistic, however, and associations are often viewed negatively as being undemocratic veto groups, as preventing the expression of legitimate opinion by individuals and unorganized groups, as eroding the broad representation of political parties, and as being too powerful in relation to elected public officials. Each of the broadest of these concerns has its counterpart in the study of higher education associations.

Studies of higher education associations demonstrate that association participants feel considerable ambiguity about the virtues of multiple and overlapping memberships and activities. On the one hand, some are convinced that each type of higher education institution and each major part of colleges and universities (faculty, presidents, students, trustees, and so on) need special representation nationally, and pressure to organize Washington-based associations for more specific and stronger representation is never absent.

An equally firm belief exists, however, that multiple and overlapping memberships are a major problem for the national system and are likely to result in exorbitant costs for the institutions that support them financially. These costs include dues, duplication and fragmentation of effort, and the creation of ruinous competition among types and parts of institutions of higher education, reflecting James Madison's views on the evils of factionalism rather than those of the mid-twentieth century advocates of a benign pluralism (Coser 1956; Lipset 1960).

The voluntary association as a buffer between the state and the individual (institution) finds expression in higher education in the preoccupation of institutional leaders with the problems of government regulation. The associations have played an important and aggressive role in tempering what has been seen as unwarranted federal incursions upon institutional autonomy, particularly in the 1970s (Bailey 1978). The buffering role is further expressed in what some associations and professional organizations do with regard to accreditation and in the peer system of reviewing proposals for federally funded research to further guarantee the degree of autonomy that higher education associations seek.

In the literature and in everyday higher education association life, the question is not so much whether genuine democratic governance structures are required for democracy to survive. Instead, the focus is on whether the association is democratic enough internally to satisfy an individual institution's sense that its concerns are listened to and its interests are sufficiently and clearly represented to the federal government and to the public. The focus invariably reduces to some version of Michels's "Iron Law of Oligarchy" (1915), that is, to the issue of what to do about the perceived inevitability that a small group of persons eventually takes control over the decision-making appara-

The associations have played an important and aggressive role in tempering . . . unwarranted federal incursions upon institutional autonomy.

tus of the association, no matter how formally democratic and egalitarian the association. This question is a serious one for association life, for higher education associations are organized democratically, with strong presumptions of equality among members, regular elections of officials, and decision-making power in the hands of the membership.

This question is submerged among the institutionally based associations, perhaps because association leaders and staff members in those associations take great pains to allay members' apprehensions concerning oligarchical inevitability. But the problem surfaces from time to time in the charge that some types of institutional interests are promoted with greater zeal and more association resources than others. The grand umbrella association, the American Council on Education, is particularly visible when such complaints arise, and it expends considerable time and effort in persuading members that such assertions are groundless.

Among the learned societies, the "democracy versus Iron Law" controversy is pervasive, continual, and often on the surface. For members of learned societies, it takes the form of a persistent belief that a ruling oligarchy, unfairly selected and maintained, dominates decision making in the association (Somit and Tanenhaus 1964). It is especially difficult in learned societies to deal with the issue of oligarchy because the disciplinary learned societies, in the midst of their formal egalitarian democratic organization, are in fact comprised of highly productive scholarly elites whose leading figures do indeed populate the offices and committees of major associations and dominate the journals and presentations at annual meetings, leaving in their wake a nonpublishing, almost non-participating proletariat. The two classes are concentrated in quite different types of colleges and universities. What gives the notion of oligarchy its particular bite in learned societies is the conviction that the same elite who get elected to offices and monopolize convention presentations control the discipline as well as the association and determine, perhaps unfairly, which kinds of research are appropriate, what should be published in association journals, and who should participate in the annual meetings. Here the problems of democracy and the Iron Law of Oligarchy are seen as connecting directly with the reward system of higher education, particularly with that system's legitimacy (Bloland and Bloland 1974).

More important for this monograph is the role of associations in giving voice to and in representing higher education, particularly in Washington, D.C. But first, let us look at how associations are created and grow and why people join them and stay in them or get out.

The Formation of Associations

Considerable interest has been expressed in recent years in the life cycles of organizations (Kimberly, Miles, and Associates 1980) and in the significance of organizational environments for the creation, growth, maintenance, and general survival of organizations (Aldrich and Pfeffer 1976). Associations are subject to the same structural and operational limitations as any other organization, so much of the literature on organizational life cycles and environments is of interest for several reasons. First, the environmental conditions at the time of the organization's creation so influence its character and structure that many of the central attributes of that organization continue to survive long after the environment has changed (Stinchcombe 1965).

Second, the creation of associations does not occur in regular, predictable patterns. "The formation of associations tends to occur in waves" (Truman 1955, p. 59), and higher education associations are no exception. At some times, many associations are created; at other periods, few are formed. The same statement is true of the move to the nation's capital, which poses a problem for those higher education associations already in Washington. They see the proliferation of associations as fragmenting the higher education community and creating conditions in which federal administrators and members of Congress may hear only a babel of voices from higher education, attenuating the effectiveness of the higher education community as a whole in Washington.

What causes associations to be formed? Those interested in the formation of interest groups emphasize three societal processes: complexity (proliferation), disturbance (Hrebener and Scott 1982, p. 110), and entrepreneurship (Kimberly 1980; McClelland 1965; Salisbury 1969; Schumpeter 1934, 1947).

First, as societies grow and become technically and socially more complex and specialized, associations are created to represent those specialized interests. The more specialized and differentiated the interests, the greater the increase in associations to represent those interests.

Since the late 1800s, American higher education has grown and diversified in spurts and jumps related to wars, depressions, prosperity, changes in public policy, and other societal changes. The uneven growth patterns have been accompanied by uneven proliferation of associations, with the increasing complexity and specialization of the higher education system producing an environment particularly conducive to the formation of new higher education associations. Higher education interests divide along such dimensions as academic level (graduate schools, two- and four-year colleges), academic emphasis (liberal arts colleges, professional schools, vocational and technical institutions), religious and nonreligious differences (Catholic, Protestant, and secular institutions), and sources of support and control (public versus private, local, state, or federal support). And, it seems, each type of higher education institution has an organized association to serve its specialized needs.

In addition, size and specialization have increased *within* higher education institutions, both in administration and among the faculty, encouraging the establishment of appropriate professional associations and learned societies to articulate the shared concerns of each institutional group.

Second, the disturbance theory assumes that the various parts of society naturally seek a state of stable relations with the environment as a whole and with other relevant associations. Changes in the society, however, ranging from innovations in technology to business cycles to changes in the federal law, produce environments in which some groups become newly disadvantaged and others advantaged. The advantaged may seek to consolidate their new positions and the disadvantaged to return to their former statuses through the organization of formalized interest groups that seek to mobilize resources and become influential (Hrebener and Scott 1982, p. 11).

Third, entrepreneurial theory explains the formation of associations as the result of the drive and ambition of one or a few persons to construct a viable association. The entrepreneur is a "person who exploits . . . an untried possibility by launching a new enterprise" (Wilson 1973). The entrepreneur takes risks and is willing to endure uncertainty and to postpone immediate gratification for success in achieving long-term goals. Such a person has a solid sense of purpose and a long-term perspective. The entrepreneur's tasks are to discover or construct a distinctive place in the sun and to identify for the organization a recognized jurisdiction (Wilson 1973, p. 204). The entrepreneur must recognize the appropriate "environmental niche" in which the association can fit snugly, that is, to organize for the association that "set of combinations of necessary resources to sustain a specific organizational population" (Brittan and Freeman 1980, pp. 318–19).

In this formation of associations and establishment of organizational niches, an entrepreneur is immeasurably aided if he or she has the support of motivated and interested cadres, that is, of small groups of people who are willing to work hard to set up the organization and to run it.

Association Membership: Why Members Join and Why They Stay or Exit

For the institutional representatives to the national associations, salient questions arise concerning membership. Why join any particular national higher education association? Why remain a member? These questions are particularly important in periods like the present, when institutions must be extremely conscious of the costs and benefits to be derived from membership. Are the benefits of membership sufficient to justify the cost of dues? Are the benefits of multiple memberships complementary or repetitious? Does the membership payment account for a substantial, visible item in an institution's operation budget?

Two theoretical perspectives have dominated systematic inquiry into why prospective members join associations and why members remain in them: the pluralistic model and the collective action model (Olson 1971).

The pluralists claim that people join groups in order to support group goals, while Olson counters that people join in response to private (selective) benefits that are typically nonpolitical (Moe 1981, p. 531).

The pluralistic perspective (probably that of most presidents of universities and colleges) asserts that institutions join and stay in associations that reflect their institutional interests; institutional members assume that the role of the association's leadership is to produce and sustain a set of cohesive goals that the appropriate institutions can and will support. Rationally, if the association does not reflect the interests of the institution, that college or university will drop out of the association.

Olson, however, asserts that rational prospective members would not join an association merely on the basis of sharing an association's goals (Olson 1971). He argues that most association goals are in the form of "collective goods," which means that they involve a "good" that, if obtained, would benefit everyone in the relevant class of persons or institutions involved and not just those who are members of the association. Therefore, he argues, powerful reasons explain why potential members would rationally choose not to participate in the collective action of joining and participating in an association. Two in particular are strong arguments against pluralism.

First, the most significant obstacle to collective action is perhaps the "free rider" problem, which seems to be inherently involved in receiving collective benefits. Each participant knows that if the collective good is supplied, any particular person (or institution) will receive the benefit as well as those who are members of the association. Thus, why cooperate with the others? In fact, why join the association in the first place?

Second, if the membership is large enough, it becomes apparent to each participant that an individual contribution to collective action will have no perceivable consequence in obtaining the collective good. Although this generalization has exceptions (for example, large members may get so much benefit from a collective good that they find it worthwhile to contribute, even independently, and, if the groups are small enough, every member can see that his or her individual contribution will make a difference), these principles logically so discourage rational collective action based upon the glue of group interest that prospective members will (or should) join associations *only* if they are offered something more than shared political and organizational goals (Olson 1971). Rationally, the incentives for joining and staying in associations must be a result of the associations' ability to offer the members "selective benefits," that is, "tangible private benefits (e.g., newsletters, attractive insurance rates, travel discounts, etc.), which can be given to association members and withheld from those who are not" (Moe 1981, p. 534). Thus, those members who join associations to get selective benefits may, and often do, continue to stay in the associations even if they do not support the organization's goals—so long as the selective benefits continue to attract them.

Although Olson's critique of the pluralist explanation of why people or institutions join and stay in associations is persuasive, his argument is flawed as well. Basically, its restrictive assumptions, that prospective members are always driven by rational economic self-interest and have at their command complete information, do not conform to what we now know about how people operate in everyday life. The concept of "perception of efficacy" has been offered as an alternate explanation. Individuals may join groups if they subjectively calculate that their participation makes a difference in achieving the group's goals or political outcomes, even if it appears from others' perspectives that no such conclusions are warranted or justified by the objective situation (Moe 1981, p. 536).

This explanation means that leadership must provide a mixture of political and nonpolitical inducements to the members to maintain the organization. It also means that in actuality people join and stay in organizations because of the association's provision of selective benefits for members *and* because of the association's ability to make available collective benefits for members and others as well.

This emphasis on the role of leadership in an association unites the importance of the entrepreneur in the formation of associations with the significance of the entrepreneur in attracting and keeping members. This leadership role is illuminated by a conceptualization of interest groups called "exchange theory" (Salisbury 1969). This theoretical posture conceives of association leaders as akin to business entrepreneurs, people who initiate activity or form organizations and offer "products" (incentives/benefits) to "customers"

This explanation means that leadership must provide a mixture of political and nonpolitical inducements to the members to maintain the organization.

(potential and current members) for a "price" (joining and staying in the association) (Salisbury 1969, p. 1).

Three basic types of incentives figure into the calculus of prospective and actual members: material, purposive, and solidary (Wilson 1973, chap. 3).

Material incentives

Material incentives correspond to Olson's nonpolitical selective benefits that induce individuals to join and stay in organizations—newsletters, insurance, advice, and information, for example. But material incentives can also refer to the tangible, political benefits that accrue to members as a result of the association's successful attempts to achieve legislative change and favorable federal, judicial, and administrative decisions.

Although higher education associations rely on all three types of incentives, material benefits are predominant, visible, and important. Higher education associations provide newsletters, training programs, conferences, journals, and information. They organize and pursue activities intended to influence members of Congress and the executive and judicial branches of the federal government.

The conflicts that arise internally in a utilitarian association (one that relies upon material incentives primarily) relate to the distribution of the material benefits. During the late 1960s, for example, some association members in the American Council on Education complained that they did not share adequately with the Big Six in Washington in the distribution of executive and legislative information gathered by the Council (Bloland and Wilson 1971).

Purposive incentives

If an association relies primarily on its stated goals or purposes to attract and keep members, it is using purposive incentives. Purposive benefits do not aid the individual association members directly, but they aid the association collectively (Hrebener and Scott 1982, p. 19). Some of the stated goals of higher education associations seem to indicate that these organizations do rely on stated goals to appeal to members. The stated goal for the American Council on Education, for example, is "to advance education and educational methods through comprehensive voluntary and cooperative action" (ACE 1969, p. 1).

Purposive incentives are often somewhat vague, as is advancing education through cooperation, causing some problems for the organization. The stated goals have to be ones that separate the association from other groups but do not create conflict among the members (Wilson 1973). Purposive incentives are important to higher education associations, but they are not as significant in the actual operation of associations as material incentives.

Solidary incentives

Solidary incentives are also intangible; they refer to such benefits as the warmth, congeniality, and enjoyment that may result from participation in the association (collective incentives) and the specific rewards of election and/or appointment to office and honors (both selective incentives). Higher education associations provide such incentives, and they may be important for the membership.

Organizations may change over time, from primarily using one type of incentive to emphasizing another. For many years the Association of American Universities was a fairly small organization whose institutional representatives, the presidents of prestigious universities, knew each other quite well. Meetings of the AAU were reportedly convivial affairs in which presidents, who ordinarily have no one on the home campus to whom they can bare their souls, let their hair down and talked freely about their problems to their understanding fellow presidents. In recent years, however, because presidents stay in office for shorter periods of time, the turnover in AAU membership reduced the possibilities for the old, strong solidary incentives. The singular pressure to which the 50 most prestigious research universities were prone changed the association from a major user of solidary incentives to an organization emphasizing the provision of material benefits for its members, as evidenced most directly by the leaders' decision to become actively engaged in federal relations.

Thus, higher education associations, much like other organizations, rely on leadership to provide a variety of incentives to attract and retain members. These incentives can be characterized as selective and collective, political and nonpolitical, tangible and intangible. In fact, the role of leadership in associations has been illuminated by seeing the relationship between leaders and members of associations in terms of the Washington higher education association world.

THE WASHINGTON-BASED EDUCATION ASSOCIATION COMMUNITY AND ITS ENVIRONMENT

The higher education association world is comprised of a wide variety of national, state, and local organizations. At the national level, higher education associations with offices at One Dupont Circle in Washington, D.C., number approximately 60. The precise number is difficult to state because associations' jurisdictions overlap and because higher education has numerous definitions. As a result of the sheer number of associations and the number of interests they represent, the Washington higher education community appears endlessly fragmented and anarchic. "Probably no other segment of American Society has so many organizations and is yet so unorganized as higher education" (Babbidge and Rosenzweig 1962, p. 92).

Demystifying Variety and Fragmentation: Classification Schemes

Those who write about the presence of higher education associations in Washington are pressed to make sense out of "the bewildering variety of education interests in the Washington area" (Bailey 1975, p. 6) by dividing the associations and placing them in meaningful categories. None of the classification schemes are satisfactory, however, because the system itself is not tidy: Interests, purposes, members, and activities overlap, combine, and divide in ways that defy neat, orderly categorization.

Nevertheless, classification schemes are necessary as a basis for discussing associations and the national system in Washington. Associations can be grouped by their primary interests and purposes: (1) institutionally tied associations (for example, the Association of American Universities), which seek to advance educational institutions as a whole or parts of them (the Council of Graduate Schools, for example); (2) learned societies (the American Sociological Association) and research associations (the American Educational Research Association), which seek to advance knowledge in the disciplines in a general area; (3) faculty organizations (the American Association of University Professors), which attempt to enhance the autonomy and the occupational state of academic faculties; (4) special task associations (accreditation associations), which are organized to perform specific functions for higher education, such as accreditation; and (5) student organizations (the National Student Association) (Bloland 1969a).

FIGURE 1
WASHINGTON-BASED EDUCATION ASSOCIATIONS:
TYPOLOGY AND EXAMPLES

- **Umbrella organizations**
  American Council on Education
  Committee for Full Funding of Education Programs

- **Institutional associations**
  American Association of Community and Junior
    Colleges
  Association of Independent Colleges and Schools

- **Teachers unions**
  National Education Association of the United States
  American Federation of Teachers
  American Association of University Professors

- **Professions, fields, and disciplines**
  Music Educators National Conference
  American Political Science Association
  Association of American Medical Colleges

- **Librarians, suppliers, and technologists**
  American Library Association
  National Audio-Visual Association, Inc.
  College Entrance Examination Board

Perhaps the broadest, most inclusive classification plan is the taxonomy that includes not only higher education associations but also elementary and secondary associations and noneducational groups that affect the Washington educational scene (see figure 1). The overall context of this scheme is educational representation in Washington (Bailey 1975).

Zeroing In on the Big Six (or Seven)
More specifically related to this monograph is the classification scheme of Lauriston King (1975), later refined by Michael Murray (1976), which emphasizes an association grouping called "the major associations" (called the "core lobbies" by Murray) and informally referred to as the "Big

FIGURE 1 (continued)

- **Religion, race, sex**
  National Catholic Educational Association
  Washington Research Project Action Council
  American Association of University Women

- **"Lib-lab" (liberal, labor) lobbies**
  AFL/CIO
  National Farmers Union

- **Institutions and institutional systems**
  Pennsylvania State University
  New York State Education Department

- **Administrators and boards**
  American Association of School Administrators
  National School Boards Association
  Association of Governing Boards of Universities and
    Colleges
  Council of Chief State School Officers

- **Miscellaneous**
  Council for Basic Education
  National Committee for Citizens in Education
  National Student Lobby

Source: Bailey 1975, p. 9.

Six." This core group of higher education associations consists of an umbrella association, the American Council on Education (ACE), and five institution-based associations—the National Association of State Universities and Land-Grant Colleges (NASULGC), the American Association of State Colleges and Universities (AASCU), the Association of American Colleges (AAC) (until 1976), the Association of American Universities (AAU), and the American Association of Community and Junior Colleges (AACJC). The central focus of this paper is upon these core associations and on the National Association of Independent Colleges and Universities (NAICU), which substituted for AAC in 1976. All of these associations are housed in the National Center for Higher Education at One

Dupont Circle, except AAC and NAICU, which are near Dupont Circle and Capitol Hill, respectively.

These six or seven associations are of most interest because they "take part most regularly and on the widest range of political concerns of all the Washington-based higher education associations" (King 1975, p. 19).

The American Council on Education

Of the six core members of the Washington higher education community, the largest and most broadly representative is ACE. Its membership in 1983 included national and regional associations, organizations, and institutions of higher education and affiliated institutions and organizations.

The Council was founded in 1918 by 14 national education associations as the Emergency Council on Education, a "peak" organization for those constituent associations. The Council's purpose was to assist in coordinating associations. After the war, the name was changed to the American Council on Education and its areas of interest and activity broadened.*

After World War I, it became apparent that ACE as an association of independent associations had no real control over those associations. It found itself handicapped in the coordination of associations. As a result and because its financial resources were meager, the Council began to organize itself to relate more directly to colleges and universities and to reduce its dependency upon its members. Although this move created conflict with some of the Council's members, ACE successfully underwent a major reorganization through a series of constitutional changes. In 1962, the Council added direct, dues-paying institutional members, forbade any decision-making assembly within the Council comprised of constituent members, and created a governing board comprised almost entirely of presidents representing their own institutions rather than representatives of constituent associations.

The Council also shifted its role from that of a coordinator of association activity and defined its role as a coordinating agency in the higher education system as a whole. This shift could be accomplished through its comprehensive membership of associations, institutions, and other

*ACE, brochure.

organizations; through its attempts to coordinate the formation of policy on the national issues and problems of higher education; and through the large number of knowledgeable people it could recruit, primarily from the institutions of higher education, to participate on the Council's board, commissions, and committees. The Council has repeatedly been asked how it can be called an "umbrella" organization with coordinating functions, when it is so often viewed as an institutionally based association competing with other institutionally based associations. Those associations called for representation on the ACE board in the 1960s. At that time, ACE's president, Logan Wilson, indicated that because many ACE board members were also members of the associations, those associations were already represented on the board. AAC and NASULGC, however, did not always find that answer satisfactory.

The coordinating role has been a difficult one to clarify, and the Council, usually through its president, has often attempted to define it.[2] Coordination is a key word in the Washington higher education community, and it must be clarified because its meaning changes in Washington. Because the associations are autonomous, they need to identify and represent their specialized constituencies, but at the same time they need to act together on some issues and activities.

The Council was caught in the problems of the 1950s that all the associations experienced, which made the activity of coordination difficult. The practice was to ask constituents how they felt about, for example, what Congress was doing. The membership took a long time to answer, and sometimes they were asked only during the associations' annual conferences. The result was that higher education often had no position on significant topics (Babbidge and Rosenzweig 1962).

The National Association of State Universities and Land-Grant Colleges

The National Association of State Universities and Land-Grant Colleges has a membership of 144 colleges, universi-

Coordination is a key word in the Washington higher education community.

---

2. The president of ACE is its chief administrative officer, chosen by the board after consultation with the membership. The chief elected official is the chair of the board.

---

ties, and state higher education systems. NASULGC is the oldest institutionally based higher education association in the United States with its roots in the Association of American Agricultural Colleges (established in 1887) and the National Association of State Universities (1895). These two associations, with the State Universities Association (founded in 1918), combined membership to produce NASULGC, which assumed its present form in 1963. Almost one-third of all higher education students in the United States are enrolled in NASULGC colleges and universities, and almost two-thirds of doctoral degrees awarded are awarded by state and land-grant institutions.*

NASULGC's primary mission has been to support high-quality and low-cost public higher education. It has a strong orientation toward promoting graduate study and research and a long-standing commitment to the use of institutional grants from the federal government. NASULGC has the reputation as an effective association in Washington. It derives its perceived strength primarily from the prestige and political skills of many of the presidents of the state universities and land-grant colleges and its long history of the land-grant schools' political experience at the state level. NASULGC has had a full-time Washington office since 1947, which has been staffed by a succession of able executive directors.

Although various vice presidents, deans, and other administrators participate in the governance of the association, NASULGC is a presidentially based association. Legislation and policy making are in the hands of the association's Senate and Senate Executive Committee. The structure of NASULGC consists of a variety of councils, commissions, divisions, and offices that reflect the association's concerns in governmental relations, relations among members, international programs, agricultural, urban, and marine affairs, research and graduate study, and the problems and concerns of historically black colleges (including the 17 land-grant institutions in this category in the association).

*AASCU 1984, brochure.

The Association of American Colleges

The Association of American Colleges was founded in 1915
by a group of independent, church-related institutions.
Although formally committed to the promotion of higher
education in general, it was for a long time the major voice
of the independent sector of higher education, with seven-
eighths of its membership of more than 800 colleges and
universities privately controlled institutions. It came to be
the leading voice for liberal arts education for four-year
colleges, both public and private. In the mid-1970s, it
expanded its membership to include other institutions (for
example, community colleges with strong commitments to
undergraduate liberal education).

The association was characterized for many years as an
organization opposed to federal aid and federal regulation
in any form. In the 1960s, it held positions similar to other
national higher education associations on most issues, but
it began separating itself from the public institutions over
the question of tax credits. AAC schools saw tax credits as
a nongovernmentally controlled means for increasing
tuition levels, a way that would provide support for institutions without raising the issue of church versus state. The
public institutions and their associations, particularly
NASULGC and AASCU, totally opposed tax credits for
personal expenditures on education.

In the 1970s, the deteriorating financial position of the
small, independent colleges created major problems for
AAC in its posture toward external relations. This situation
led to a series of internal changes designed to reconcile the
needs of independent colleges in terms of financial and federal relations with the thrusts of liberal education. It culmi-
nated in a series of crises that resulted in the formation of a
new organization within the association and ultimately to
the organization of a separate association to represent private higher education, leaving AAC to dedicate itself to the
promotion of liberal education.

The American Association of State Colleges and Universities

The membership of AASCU is comprised of more than 350
state colleges and universities. Many of these institutions
are former teacher training institutions. Others started as
municipal universities and community colleges or as agri-

cultural and technical schools. Some members are recently established comprehensive institutions.* Twenty percent of the 12 million students enrolled in higher education in the United States attend colleges and universities that belong to AASCU; the institutions represented by AASCU award almost one-third of the undergraduate degrees in the United States.

AASCU was founded in 1961 and established a Washington office in 1962. Its president, Allan Ostar, is the dean of the chief executive officers of the Washington higher education associations, having been head of the AASCU offices in Washington since its inception.

AASCU has maintained close ties with the land-grant and community college associations and has worked closely with ACE. It is noted for providing a wide range of services for its members. In addition to its representative function in Washington, AASCU analyzes federal and state programs and is involved in international education through its promotion of internationalization of curricula and its encouragement of opportunities for exchange programs for scholars and technical assistance. The association conducts workshops and seminars and publishes materials on a range of topics, such as professional development, future planning, program evaluation, and partnerships with local governments. AASCU seeks to connect its member institutions with business, labor, and public affairs. Like NASULGC, the organization supports policies that encourage low tuition and is committed to equal opportunity in higher education. It joins a number of other higher education associations in Washington in strongly advocating increases for student assistance programs, but AASCU finds itself at odds with associations representing the independent sector in its opposition to several provisions of the Pell grants. AASCU, for example, supports the elimination of the provision in the Pell grants that limits the amount of a student's award to 50 percent of the cost of his education.† AASCU supported the commuter allowance of the Pell grant program and also supports federal aid to part-time students, science education bills, and federal aid to science and technology in general.

*AASCU 1984, brochure.
†NASULGC 1984, brochure.

American Association of Community and Junior Colleges
The American Association of Community and Junior Colleges was established in 1920 as an association of junior colleges. It now represents the interests of 1,219 community, technical, and junior colleges. The mission of the AACJC stresses advocacy of community colleges' interests in Washington and elsewhere and service in the form of widely diverse programs for its members. The organization is a product of the historically ambiguous place of the two-year college in higher education in the United States. The community and junior college movement has needed to establish a readily perceived identity and to make that identity known to its constituents. In Washington, it has taken the form of strong, aggressive advocacy for community colleges to Congress and the federal agencies. AACJC is also known for its willingness and ability to realistically modify its positions on issues, however.

AACJC has also been active in relating to governors, state legislators, and business and labor leaders. The association allies itself quite naturally with AASCU and NASULGC in representing the public sector of higher education and advocating low tuition. Ninety percent of the students attending its member schools are enrolled in public institutions. It departs from NASULGC in having little interest in graduate education and support for research. In fact, the way in which dwindling federal dollars are divided among research support, graduate education, and undergraduate student aid is a potential source of conflict in the public sector.

Ever since AACJC moved to Washington, it has maintained a large organizational presence (though quite small in comparison to labor unions and business associations) and since 1970 has had an office staff of about 60 people, making it second only to the American Council on Education in the size of its office and the range of its activities.

AACJC has its own particular areas of concern that have set it apart from some of the other associations. At one time, these special interests, combined with strong growth and support from the grass roots (every congressional district, it was said, has at least one community college in it), led the association to contemplate going its own way as a third education sector, somewhere between elementary and secondary education and higher education. In recent years, however, this idea has diminished. Still, the association's interest in vocational education, education in the semiprofessions, technical training, adult education, and community service makes it a special advocate in higher education.

Association of American Universities

The Association of American Universities is a relatively small association whose members consist primarily of the most prestigious private and public institutions in the United States and Canada. Its interests focus on support of graduate education and large-scale research and the associated issues. For most of its history, it acted as the quintessential "president's club." Presidents met twice a year in private sessions with no printed proceedings as they discussed the common concerns of university presidents. As an association it was not active, even after it organized a small office in Washington in 1962. Part of its reticence in Washington is believed to have been a result of the high level of direct access to Washington decision makers that the individual presidents had. In addition, its leaders believed that if they spoke infrequently, when they did speak their testimony would be more effective (Bloland 1969a). According to an AAU spokesman:

> There is a tendency in AAU to believe you can exhaust yourself by testifying too much. If you speak out too much, you are not listened to. . . . AAU prefers not to exhaust its leverage by speaking out on too many issues (King 1975, p. 90).

The Satellites

The second group of associations has been named "the special interest associations" (King 1975, p. 29) and the "satellite lobbies" (Murray 1976, p. 83). While whole institutions are members of the major associations, the satellite associations represent specialized groups that are parts of whole institutions and smaller, more specialized colleges and universities. They become involved in policy issues that specifically affect them but for the most part let the major associations take the lead and represent their interests. These satellite associations are subdivided into two groups, based upon the associations they orbit.

One cluster, identified in 1970, is comprised of associations with major interests in research and in graduate and professional programs (for example, the Council of Graduate Schools in the U.S., the Association of American Medical Colleges, and the Association of American Law Schools). Their interests link them to members of NASULGC and AAU that are deeply involved in the same activities. Because many associations in this satellite group have strong connections with specialized professional clientele, they are likely to relate more closely with the appropriate professional associations (the American Medical Association and the American Bar Association, for example) than with the appropriate core associations (King 1975, p. 29). Initially, these satellite associations did not as a rule become involved in the issues that engaged the attention of whole institutions, but in recent years, some of the satellites have been more involved in mainstream concerns because of the great increase in federal legislation that affects them all, particularly federal regulatory practices and activities.

Another group of satellite associations has close links to the Association of American Colleges. These organizations represent special kinds of institutions, particularly colleges with religious affiliations and colleges of marginal status and financial condition (King 1975, p. 29). They include the college and university departments of the National Catholic Educational Association, the Council of Protestant Colleges and Universities (since dissolved), and the Council for the Advancement of Private Independent Four-Year Institutions (p. 30).

Since King and Murray classified associations in 1975 and 1976, however, the position of AAC and its relationship to other associations has changed considerably, with new associations emerging from their traditional constituencies. NAICU has emerged as the center of a group of associations from the independent sector that link directly to NAICU through a secretariat.

Beyond the satellite associations is a pattern of institutional representation involving state systems (for example, the State University of New York), single institutions (for example, Ohio State University, which has an office in Washington), predominantly black colleges (College Service Bureau), and regional consortia (Associated Colleges of the Midwest) (King 1975, pp. 30–32). Murray calls this group the "peripheral lobbies" (1976, p. 84) and extends this group to include the learned societies (the American Political Science Association, for example), occupational groups with specialized constituencies (the National Association of Admissions Officers), and special task groups (the Brookings Institution), which sometimes line up with the core and satellite groups. In addition, some private entrepreneurs, for a profit, will guide clients to funding sources and advise them on grant proposals (King 1972).

Although a number of the relationships among associations and between associations and the federal government have changed and new associations have been created that participate in the Washington higher education community, the classification of associations into three general categories is still relevant: (1) a core group heavily involved in political concerns of interest to higher education associations; (2) a satellite group of associations that rely greatly on the major associations to represent their interests but participate when their specialized interests are at issue; and (3) a peripheral group whose members exist primarily to provide services to their constituents and stay away from politics.

The Policy Arena
The higher education associations are but one part of a larger higher education policy arena in Washington. A policy arena is comprised of "political actors [who] usually . . . perceive their policy-making activities and interests in terms of a cluster of issues that are substantially related to each other" (Gladieux and Wolanin 1976, p. 251). The higher education policy arena is distinguished from other arenas because it pays "attention to issues and federal programs that aim at fostering and expanding opportunities in higher education" (p. 251). Thus, it focuses on three types of programs and issues:

> . . . first, student aid administered by the Office of Education for undergraduate and graduate students; second, institution building programs such as college housing and higher education facilities; and third, categorical programs to improve the quality of instruction in

general, or for selected higher education clientele, such as librarians (Gladieux and Wolanin 1976, p. 251).

Student aid is the most important, and substantive legislation is involved—the National Defense Education Act of 1958, the Higher Education Facilities Act of 1963, the Higher Education Act of 1965, and the Education Amendments of 1972.

Another part of the policy arena includes the long-term, fairly stable relationships among the appropriate congressional committees and staffs, departments, bureaus, agencies, interest groups—particularly the Washington higher education associations—and clienteles. This network of relationships has been termed a "subgovernment" (Gladieux and Wolanin 1976, p. 252), which consisted a decade ago of the higher education units (especially the Office of Education) in the Department of Health, Education, and Welfare, the Postsecondary Education Subcommittee of the House of Representatives, a subcommittee on education of the Senate, and the Washington higher education representatives (p. 252).

The 1960s witnessed a series of events that made the policy arena possible. First, the Office of Education, which had been a sleepy, rather passive organization for most of its existence, grew rapidly in response to its responsibility for administering the federal education programs of the late 1950s and 1960s. The executive branch distinguished higher education by creating an "assistance for higher education" category in the budget in 1963 (Gladieux and Wolanin 1976). In 1957, a Special Committee on Education was created; it eventually became the Subcommittee on Postsecondary Education. Proposals for higher education began to be considered separately from other proposals for education. A survey of federal government higher education activities was undertaken in the House, and an ad hoc committee to investigate higher education was appointed by Representative Adam Clayton Powell, then the head of the Education and Labor Committee. The Senate did not change its organization to distinguish higher education concerns from those of other education groups, but Senator Claiborne Pell became a significant actor in higher education policy.

The 1960s witnessed a series of events that made the policy arena possible.

Higher education associations had been in existence long before the 1960s; NASULGC, for example, was created in 1887 in its initial form. Only four of the Big Six had offices in Washington by 1950, however, and the six core associations as a group did not operate in Washington until 1962. In addition, in 1962, the executive secretaries of the Big Six and five other associations formed the Washington Higher Education Secretariat, a group comprised of the executive secretaries of the eleven associations. The Secretariat held monthly meetings to discuss issues and ideas, particularly in the area of federal education policy. Much of the structure was in place when most of the principal associations moved to One Dupont Circle, which became the National Center for Higher Education in 1968.

This policy arena, as a coherent system, emerged in the 1960s, and its institutionalization was more or less complete by the 1970s. Although many of the individual actors have changed, the basic legislation has been extended, modified, and added to, and new issues and concerns have broadened the scope of what Washington associations must pay attention to, this policy arena is still basically intact in the 1980s. Many of the actors are part of what has been called the ''liberal consensus'' in higher education (Finn 1980). Despite the crisis that is alleged to have cracked this consensus and the efforts of President Reagan and some top administration officials to cut back and eliminate higher education programs and the Education Department, that liberal consensus still seems dominant in Congress (particularly in the House of Representatives), in the Washington higher education associations, and perhaps in the Education Department itself (although personnel changes there may eventually turn it into a citadel of conservatism).

The Higher Education Act of 1965 and the Amendments of 1972, with subsequent modifications, are still the legislative anchors of the policy arena (student aid remains the central consideration), even though they have now been joined by a considerable number of essentially regulatory laws. To understand the contexts within which higher education decisions are made at the federal level, one can refer to some good, somewhat similar frameworks (Gladieux and Wolanin 1976; Schuster 1982).

The primacy of the states

Much of the reason for the reluctance of higher education associations to become aggressively engaged at the national level has been the almost universal assumption that the division of powers between the federal government and the states put the federal government in a secondary, supporting role in relation to the states (for both higher and lower education). This assumption has affected not only how other institutions would allow associations to participate at the federal level but also the thinking of the higher education associations and the institutions' leadership. Federal expenditures as recently as 1979–80 were about 16.5 percent of the revenues of independent colleges and universities and somewhat over 11 percent for public institutions of higher education (Schuster 1982, p. 584). The Constitution, except for the First and Fourteenth Amendments, does not bar the federal government from participating in higher education to a much greater or lesser degree than it now does. It has discretion. The federal limits on participation in higher education are really political and pragmatic. "The federal role in education is defined by the will of the polity" (p. 584).

Instrumental view of higher education

> Scholarship, research, and creativity for their own sake have never enjoyed great favor with the American public and with federal policy makers. Higher education instead has historically had the support of the general public as well as the federal government because it is "useful" (Gladieux and Wolanin 1976, p. 4).

Nowhere in the period from World War I to 1968 did higher education appear more useful than in the service of national defense. When the federal government wanted the services of scientists from universities, for example, federal agencies contacted faculty members directly instead of going through the institutions. Institutions, wanting to protect themselves and their autonomy, thus began to attempt to influence the federal agencies through their national associations in Washington.

The assumptions held in government and by the public of the instrumental role that higher education should play are seen in the use of federal money in the universities from the 1940s through the 1960s and beyond to increase equal educational opportunity. The associations could approve and go along with these decisions—or be left out. Eventually, despite their fears that federal decision making was an invasion of the universities' decision-making powers, they cooperated with federal policy.

Public/private nondiscrimination
Over the years, while Congress and various administrations have attempted with some success to avoid favoring private higher education or public higher education, the principle that has guided federal activities in higher education has been to treat both sectors evenhandedly. It is currently very difficult to formulate legislation that does not violate the principle of evenhandedness.

Fragmentation of federal higher education policy
Generally, it is assumed that the federal government does not have a policy on higher education; in fact, however, federal departments, agencies, and bureaus have missions, and they have provided resources to higher education to help them further their own missions. Thus, associations have not dealt with a single powerful ministry of education but with myriad federal agencies that have some interest in and capacity to make decisions concerning education. This situation has been both detrimental and beneficial to the associations.

In the Shadow of Elementary and Secondary Education: Higher Education and the Federal Government
Mass education has been a priority in the United States, so elementary and secondary education has been more important—larger, more controversial, and with more resources. Among other things, for a long time elementary and secondary education associations were more aggressive, more visible, and more listened to nationally than were higher education associations. Although the system of higher education has always been decentralized in the United States (Bloland 1969a), the trend for 200 years was toward centralization (Schuster 1982, p. 584). Only since the Reagan

administration has any calculated effort been made by a national administration to decentralize higher education. Even so, a great deal of uncalculated dispersion of decision making has been occurring nationally for some time (Schuster 1982, p. 583).

Long before the associations were organized and came to Washington—since the beginning of the republic, in fact—the federal government has been involved in higher education. Although that involvement grew in fits and starts, it was not extensive until the 1960s. For purposes of this discussion, the first most visible and notable federal action was the Morrill Act of 1862. This act was particularly significant, for it set precedents for the federal government–higher education relationship that endured at least until the 1960s. Both the federal government's instrumental view of higher education and the principle of no discrimination between private and public institutions were evident in the Morrill Act. The act provided support for the teaching and study of agriculture and mechanics, two useful subjects in which the federal government saw a national shortage, and institutions benefiting from the act did not have to be public. It also originated the grant-in-aid process. The Morrill Act stimulated the organization of the Association of American Agricultural Colleges and Experimental Stations, which eventually, along with other associations, became the National Association of State Universities and Land-Grant Colleges in 1963.

A second event that influenced the creation of a national organization was the passage of the National Defense Act in 1916, which created the Reserve Officers Training Corps that put military training on college and university campuses. It provided part of the stimulus for organizing the American Council on Education in 1918 (King 1975, p. 3).

Despite the close connections between the actions of the federal government and the organization of two higher education associations that have become active in the federal government–higher education arena, those associations and their members tended more to accommodate than to influence the federal government, at least until the late 1950s. The federal government paid almost no attention to what institutions of higher education and their associations wanted until World War II. At that time, the relationship between ACE and the federal government changed dramatically; the Council became involved in and shaped a great many federal activities, including the highly significant G.I. Bill of 1944 (Tuttle 1970). Despite this activity, however, the postwar period was clearly under the influence of the elementary and secondary education sector. The major education issues that the federal government dealt with focused on lower education, primarily desegregation and aid to private schools.

The National Defense Education Act of 1958

Although the National Defense Education Act of 1958 (NDEA) followed the long-standing federal government policy of using higher education to serve national needs for trained men and women (its instrumental view of higher education)—in this case national security—this law is also viewed as a significant breakthrough in reorienting the federal role in higher education. It included a student loan program and graduate fellowships. The actual provisions of the act were not so important, however, as its embodiment of a "psychological breakthrough."

> It asserted more forcefully than at any time in nearly a century a national interest in the quality of education that the states, communities, and private institutions provide (Sundquist 1968, p. 179).

The major impetus for passage of NDEA was the launching of *Sputnik* in 1958, and the major actors in its initiation and passage were in the administration, particularly Elliot Richardson of the Department of Health, Education, and Welfare, and Senator Lister Hill. The associations had little to do with it.

Search for an effective federal policy

Higher education associations in the decade before NDEA had exhibited a low profile, were not well organized, and were too fragmented to present a coherent approach to the federal government–higher education relationship. They did not initiate ideas about higher education legislation for the administration and Congress, and they were divided on the question of federal aid itself. The American Council on Education and other associations had been effective in turning the President's Committee on Education Beyond the High School from its anti-federal-aid stance to a pro-federal-aid stance by providing enrollment projections and cost analyses and comparing them with income projections to show the need for a new source of financial support for colleges and universities—namely, the federal government (Sundquist 1968, p. 195). But the associations did not sustain the effort to build support among their members and to bring influence to bear on government officials to obtain aid from the federal government. The associations had not been organized as lobbies to begin with, and many association members were opposed to federal aid to institutions of higher education (Babbidge and Rosenzweig 1962).

Two ways of dealing with the federal government and national issues were particularly troublesome for the associations up to the 1960s, and they detracted considerably from the associations' effectiveness. The first was a tendency on the part of the associations and their presidents to take a high policy position on broad social/political questions when they did not need to to promote their own needs. In 1960, for example, the presidents of institutions through the associations wanted to gain support for federal aid to their institutions. When higher education spokesmen

> . . . debated the possibility of aid to higher education, they were not content to describe their needs and the most effective manner of meeting them; instead they took on the larger issue, whether it would constitute sound public policy to meet these needs. They did not argue over their needs and interests; they argued over a broad question of public policy, in this instance, the church-state issue (Babbidge and Rosenzweig 1962, p. 101).

This method of operating was likely to be more true of college presidents than those who represented them in Washington.

> In many cases . . . college presidents (and it is almost always the presidents who are involved in these matters) have leaned over backwards to tackle an issue of public policy [that] they could and, from the political standpoint, probably should have avoided . . . and their voluntary pronouncements immensely complicated their

*legislative efforts. . . . There is a genuine conflict
between the role . . . they seek for themselves as educational statesmen and their role as political operators lobbying on behalf of higher education* (Rosenzweig 1965,
pp. 60–61).

The second way of interacting with the federal government that seemed to reduce the effectiveness of the Washington associations was the practice of Washington representatives' consulting their presidents to define where the
associations stood on policy questions. This inability to
take independent action meant that the Washington representatives were unable to tell congressional leaders where
higher education stood in legislative matters. Thus,
congressional leaders began to strongly request the higher
education community to organize education in Washington
so it could act with some unity and give Congress some
sense of what it wanted (King 1975, p. 74).

The associations find a cooperative mode

Senator Joseph S. Clark proposed a bill that would have
the federal government provide loans for the construction
of academic buildings (loan programs for equipment and
classrooms already existed). The associations were represented at congressional hearings on the bill but again were
divided. Private institutions were generally in favor of the
loans, but public institutions wanted grants and opposed
loans (Sundquist 1968, p. 197). The bill easily passed the
Senate and the House, but it was added to a larger housing
bill that failed to pass the House of Representatives. It was
significant that such a bill could find enough support in
both houses to pass, even though the associations gave it
little support.

By 1960, Senator Clark was displaying public displeasure
with the higher education associations. At a meeting of
organizational representatives, he proposed that a lobbying
organization be formed of all those who were committed to
federal aid and that such an association could put together
a grant proposal and work for its acceptance (Sundquist
1968, p. 200). The associations showed little response to
his suggestions, so in a speech in 1960 at a conference of
the American Assembly attended by many of the higher

education national leaders, Senator Clark gave the associations a dressing down.

> *I wonder whether existing organizations in the field of higher education are set up to do the job of working out a proper plan for federal aid and then lobbying vigorously for it* (Sundquist 1968, p. 200).

The associations this time responded quickly and put together a grant bill in less than a month, which Senator Clark then introduced in the Senate at the end of June 1960.

In the fall of 1960, the American Council on Education brought the other major associations together to work on a plan for a federally financed construction program for colleges and universities. The association representatives agreed on a combination grant and loan program in which the federal government would supply $1 billion of an estimated $2 billion worth of construction needs (Sundquist 1968, p. 202).

Three Political Perspectives

The Washington representatives frequently have "contradictory, diverse, and ambivalent" ideas about the appropriate relationship between higher education and the federal government (King 1975, p. 66). Those attitudes reflect the representative campus constituencies and how others see the relationship between higher education and the federal government. According to King, three overlapping themes characterize these political perspectives among the institutional associations. The traditional orientation proposes a small political role for higher education. The second approach, pragmatic realism, retains traditional assumptions about the diminished role of higher education but admits to the necessity for higher education to participate, however reluctantly, in political activity on behalf of its constituents, often through building coalitions, seeking consensus, and presenting a united front. The third orientation, rarely encountered in action, is the "activist perspective," which means considerably more assertiveness in national politics (King 1975, p. 65).

The following discussion draws upon King for his description of the assumptions of these three themes and places the activist perspective in the context of the period

The Washington representatives frequently have "contradictory, diverse, and ambivalent" ideas about the appropriate relationship between higher education and the federal government.

from the mid-1970s to the mid-1980s, a decade since the publication of King's book. The following discussion is thus an interpretation of King's concepts and the events and relations of the period from the 1950s to the mid-1980s.

The traditional approach

King's traditional perspective, when applied to the Big Six (plus one), includes some strong assumptions that have undergirded education's relationships, not just to government but to politics in general. First, higher education has inherent value to society and should automatically attract support from all the major sectors of society, including government (King 1975, p. 65). Second, higher education is a special enterprise that adds immeasurably to the intellectual and cultural stock of the nation just by fulfilling its missions of teaching, research, and community service—in general, its pursuit of truth and knowledge.

These assumptions have had some important political consequences. First, to guarantee the integrity of its mission, higher education should be insulated from governmental and societal controls as much as possible, and it should be outside and above the political arena. When higher education must enter politics, it should do so not for its own narrow self-interests but to address broad questions of national policy rationally and objectively. Thus, in the early 1960s, for example, in discussions of federal aid to education, university officials tended to approach the subject not in terms of their own interests or even their own needs, but to present conflicting opinions on the broad issue of church/state relations. Associations varied in their attachment to the traditional perspective; the AAC still opposed federal aid as late as 1963, for example, when almost all the other associations had accepted it as legitimate.

A second political consequence of the traditional orientation was that associations paid much attention and deference to small groups with distinctly minority views. The small Protestant colleges in the AAC, for example, were vocal and uncompromising in their opposition to federal aid to higher education institutions as late as the early 1960s, and they said so publicly in the midst of attempts to pass a higher education facilities act in 1962 (King 1975, p. 66).

A third political consequence was that the traditional perspective helped prevent higher education associations from entering coalitions with interest groups outside higher education, such as the unions, business associations, agricultural groups, and medical associations.

Pragmatic realism

The orientation of pragmatic realism was forged in the 1960s and 1970s. It was a result of attempts by Washington leaders to retain the traditional perspective while dealing with the realities of the federal government's producing financial and program legislation that greatly increased the government's role in higher education. Pragmatic realism was an attempt to face the situation realistically but not to change it drastically. The political consequence of this attempt to merge the traditional view with new realities was to perpetuate the avoidance of aggressive political action and to place much more emphasis upon building a coalition (King 1975).

The quintessential example of pragmatic realism was the associations' ambivalent posture in relation to the Emergency Committee for Full Funding of Education Programs in 1969. This committee was comprised of almost 80 education groups, and although it was dominated by the elementary and secondary education associations, it did include higher education. It attempted to unite education at all levels near the end of the Johnson presidency and during the first year of the Nixon era. The response of the higher education community varied from enthusiastic participation to hesitancy, wariness, and outright opposition.

The activist perspective

This orientation continues the assumption that higher education is indeed a special area of policy and needs to be accorded special attention and that rational decision making should predominate in the broad questions of national interest in higher education. The activists believe, however, that government and society view the special quality of higher education as less important to the national wellbeing than it once was and that higher education is in competition with other worthy interests. As a result, higher education must compete for support and thus engage directly in political activism. The basic orientation that makes this perspective different from the other two is the shift from strictly rational policy perspectives and the notion of participating in broad political discussions to the notion of an interest-oriented position that views the formation of policy as the result of the interaction of organizations seeking to express their interests. King's formulation is a reiteration of hard-nosed pluralist politics, though it is softened by his idea that this kind of politics would "redirect national priorities away from the hardware concerns of space exploration and military stakes policy to the humane concerns of health, education, and environmental policies" (King 1975, p. 79).

King's version of activism is supported more by small associations and state officials than by the larger associations. It envisioned separation of active political lobbying in the form of a single lobbying association from the community of independent associations, each with its own programmatic thrusts. Its most appealing feature was its emphasis upon the higher education associations' engaging directly in the rough and tumble world of competitive interest group politics. Its shortcoming is that it did not take the form of a higher education lobbying organization that would reconcile differences and speak for all of higher education. Thus, a more flexible, loosely coupled system emerged from the mid-1970s to the mid-1980s.

Traditional perspectives and pragmatic realism accurately reflect the orientation of association officials in the 1950s and 1960s, even into the early 1970s. The following sections scrutinize these periods and their influence in the activities of the associations as they grappled with the problem of making their associations and community voices heard in Washington.

THE 1960s: STEPS TOWARD A COOPERATING COMMUNITY

Higher education and the associations changed greatly in the 1960s. For most of the decade, student enrollments, salaries for faculty and administrators, contract research, and capital investment expanded. Public institutions grew much faster than the private schools, and community colleges mushroomed.

Several of the major controversies of the previous decade were muted in the 1960s. The issue of federal aid to private institutions, although never as significant in higher education as in elementary and secondary education, faded as private schools were included in a number of federal programs benefiting higher education—research funding, construction loans, and NDEA (Advisory Commission 1981, p. 12). Fears about federal control were attenuated when large amounts of money from the federal government became available to higher education institutions through the implementation of major legislation affecting higher education. The issue of segregation became less intense as the federal government attempted to provide equal educational opportunity to all who wished it.

Two major higher education laws were enacted during the 1960s: the Higher Education Facilities Act of 1963 and the Higher Education Act of 1965. Together, they represent a shift from the position that higher education is instrumental in national defense to an emphasis upon achieving equal educational opportunity. These two laws and the 1972 Amendments were also viewed as promoting equality at the expense of quality in higher education (Moynihan 1975), an issue that returned forcefully in the 1980s.

The Higher Education Facilities Act provided grants and loans for classrooms and other constructed facilities and allowed private and public institutions to participate (Gladieux and Wolanin 1976, p. 11). President John F. Kennedy had attempted in 1961 and 1962 to pass education bills that included loans for construction and for undergraduate scholarships. The 1961 bill included aid to elementary and secondary schools (as well as aid to higher education) and was killed because such aid was extremely controversial at that time. The 1962 bill was introduced separately from the legislation for elementary and secondary schools and almost passed. It went through both houses but was rejected at the last moment as the election neared and party identifications and the religious issue became important (Gladieux and Wolanin 1976, p. 10).

In 1964, the Equal Employment Opportunity Act and an important civil rights act were passed. Lyndon B. Johnson was elected decisively and brought large Democratic majorities to both houses. These events prepared the way for the Higher Education Act of 1965, which directly sought to carry out the growing government policy of promoting social opportunity and equal opportunity through federal law (Advisory Commission 1981, p. 23). Its major thrust was a program of scholarships for undergraduates, that is, the educational opportunity grants that were to be awarded to the financially needy. In addition to student aid, the bill contained other categorical programs dealing with grants to college libraries, the Teacher Corps, Aid to Developing Institutions, and more money for the 1963 construction programs.

In the 1960s, the initiation and formulation of educational policy was centered in the White House. Higher education associations in contrast, particularly during the Johnson years, had access to the federal policy process primarily through Congress and the bureaucracy. Thus, the higher education associations, although supportive of Johnson, felt somewhat excluded from the policy makers around the president.

The Associations' Response

During the 1960s, major associations found a cause that increasingly united them—institutional aid. The American Council on Education's 1969 statement, "Federal Programs for Higher Education: Needed Next Steps," reflected this position for the community. In part, the report read, "The principal unfinished business of the federal government in the field of higher education is the necessity to provide support for general institutional purposes" (Gladieux and Wolanin 1976, p. 41).

Although they were united on the subject, some associations were not as committed as others. Many of AAC's members still had misgivings, but this hesitancy was not as strong as in the early part of the 1960s and before. Associations could not agree about what form institutional aid should take and later how it was to be done and at what rate with benefits for whom. Two major perspectives emerged among the most important actors in the political arena. In supporting higher education, the federal government would emphasize institutional aid or direct financial help to students. Both forms of support were already in place, but a major debate concerned what the mix of institutional and student aid should be and which basic direction federal funding should reflect (Gladieux and Wolanin 1976, p. 42). The associations' united front for institutional aid illustrated the more active role that higher education associations were beginning to play in Washington.

The Creation of Community: Cooperative Mechanisms and Community Norms

The relationship between higher education and the federal government broadened in scope, speeded up, and became more intense in the 1960s. Washington representatives succeeded campus-based presidents and other college officials as the most active, knowledgeable participants in higher education on the political scene in Washington. Presidents and campus officials were not left out of the decision- and policy-making processes, however. Rather, events were moving so fast and education-related legislation and policy making were becoming so complicated that only full-time, Washington-based representatives could keep fully abreast of the changing situation.

With a group of the major, institutionally based association offices concentrated in Washington near Dupont Circle and federal relations coming to the forefront, chief executive officers and federal relations officers increased their informal interaction, and several new structures greatly enhanced communication among association officials. Most of these structures were informal social mechanisms; they were not legal entities, had no official authority, and had no decision-making power except through consensus (Bloland 1969a, p. 154).

The oldest of these informal groups, the Governmental Relations Luncheon Group (often referred to as the Tuesday Luncheon Club) met every other week for years at the Brookings Institution. Its members discussed federal and association activities. It began as a small, intimate luncheon during the Korean War, grew to about 25 members

The relationship between higher education and the federal government broadened . . . and became more intense in the 1960s.

in the mid-1960s, and continued to grow until it became so large and unwieldy that it was viewed as no longer useful to the members of the Big Six.

The luncheon club in its salad days was attended by the chief executive officers of the associations and frequently by U.S. Office of Education officials. The luncheon was the occasion for the exchange of information and discussion of controversial issues, and it sometimes served as the instrument for determining the associations' sentiment on a subject and arriving at informal consensus.

After the American Council on Education was reorganized in 1962, a group of 12 association executive directors began to meet monthly with ACE's new president, Logan Wilson. This group, the Secretariat, included representatives from the Big Six plus representatives from other associations—the Council of Protestant Colleges, the National Commission on Accreditation, and the American Association of University Professors. The participants discussed any topic of concern to them, but much of their conversation concerned federal legislation and how the associations should relate to it. The participants informed each other of their respective organizations' activities, shared interpretations of federal policy, and sought consensus on a variety of topics. When they reached consensus on occasion, responsibility for contacting appropriate legislators or government officials was given to the various associations. When the chief executive officers could not attend those meetings, no substitute association representative took their place.

The Secretariat was a most important and influential informal mechanism for coordination during the 1960s and early 1970s. It was viewed as an exclusive, powerful group whose membership included the most important organizations, the associations that could mobilize cooperative endeavors among the associations, find consensus on policy issues, and speak for higher education on those issues.

Other groups met periodically. ACE's Commission on Federal Relations, directed by John Morse (the Morse Group), consisted primarily of university presidents and chancellors who assembled several times a year to formulate policies for ACE. Morning sessions were open and became an occasion for association representatives, among others, to discuss issues that concerned the commission.

Afternoons were devoted to closed executive sessions where the commission's policies were determined. Also, for a time, the Associate Commissioner for Higher Education met with association officers about once a month to brief the associations on the Office of Education's activities and to become informed of higher education's responses to federal programs.

Community Norms

In the context of coalitions for decision making, a context involving the kind of independent organizations comprising the Washington association community, general norms prevail for the community as a whole. These norms generally are not written and are not formally binding, but most association participants tend to follow them most of the time (Warren 1967).

For the association community in Washington in the 1960s, the representatives' primary commitment was to the membership of their individual associations, which retained final authority over policy. But certain norms influenced behavior among executive officers—informal rules to which they paid attention that were not inconsistent with their responsibilities to their members.

The associations seemed to agree tacitly that legislation benefiting other associations should not be actively opposed by any other particular association. Thus, although the NASULGC groups had strongly disapproved of legislation to provide undergraduate scholarships for a long time, NASULGC did not publicly, actively oppose such legislation when much of the rest of the community favored it (Babbidge and Rosenzweig 1962).

In another case, when the AAJC Office of Governmental Affairs publicly objected to a bill that AASCU and NASULGC supported, several executive officers of associations in the community expressed disapproval directly to the American Association of Junior Colleges. No powerful sanctions were applied and expressions of disapproval were the limit of punishment for violating the community norm, but the norm did exist and it was for the most part honored.

In their need and desire to coordinate activities and orientations and to present a unified approach to federal relations, the associations also disapproved of any particular sector's attempt to be too active and too independent in obtaining special consideration for its members. Again, the president of ACE strongly reprimanded the AAJC at a Secretariat meeting because it was thought to have inappropriately urged Congress to pass legislation giving special benefits to the community and junior colleges.

Another expectation among the members of the Secretariat was that before taking major action, members would consult with the other members, even when their interests did not coincide. In fact, bases for serious disagreement always occurred, but the members exhibited genuine determination to follow the norms and inform each other.

These norms reaffirmed the community's belief that higher education would benefit most from real attempts to discover and sustain unity in its relations with the federal government. In general, the associations attempted to deemphasize areas of disagreement, to consult with each other, to seek unity, and to emphasize those areas where they agreed.

The Close of the Decade

The 1960s marked the transition from the traditional perspectives of earlier years to the organization of a community of associations that acted as a coalition on many issues. This transition to pragmatic realism involved a determined effort on the part of the associations to reach consensus on as many issues as possible, and they were successful many times.

The difference is illustrated by the remarks of two United States Senators, one at the beginning of the decade, the other after the passage of the 1965 Higher Education Act. During hearings on aid to higher education in the 1960s, Senator Clark stated:

> *I am somewhat disappointed . . . that despite the fact that the President's Committee on Education Beyond the High School made its report over three years ago, there is still no unanimity among agencies representing our higher education institutions as to what kind of help they want from the federal government. They all know they want help, but they can't agree on what form it should take. I hope that conflict will shortly be resolved* (cited in Bloland 1969a, p. 131).

By 1966, on the other hand, in hearings on the higher education amendments in the Senate, Senator Wayne Morse commented:

If one were to ask me to name the one major reason why we have been able in recent years to have a breakthrough in education legislation—with the result that since the first year of the Kennedy administration we have passed more federal aid to education legislation quantitatively and qualitatively than has been passed in the preceding 100 years . . . I would tell you that it is because at long last the educational segment of our country moved forward as a united body in support of all the various pieces of education legislation (cited in Bloland 1969a, pp. 131–32).

As the 1960s drew to a close, two events—participation in the Emergency Committee for the Full Funding of Education and the Sullivan report—indicated strongly that federal relations during the next years would become even more significant. These events were definite signs that the associations needed to find better, stronger, more workable ways to coordinate their activities, to represent their members, and to influence legislation and federal policy decisions.

The Emergency Committee for the Full Funding of Education

The emergency committee was organized in 1969, not long after Richard Nixon unveiled his first budget. Although it was not promising for higher education, even before then higher education had felt the negative effect of budget cuts from the last years of the Johnson administration and its preoccupation with Vietnam. The impetus behind the committee was that if all the education sectors were organized politically and made a united effort to back and increase funds for education, that effort would have a good chance of succeeding. By the summer of 1969, the coalition consisted of about 80 education groups representing all levels—higher education, elementary and secondary education, and vocational education. They successfully persuaded the House of Representatives to add $1 billion to the appropriation for the Office of Education. President Nixon vetoed the $19.7 billion appropriation for the Department of Labor and the Department of Health, Edu-

cation, and Welfare because, he said, the budget was infla-
tionary. At that point, the emergency committee went into
action and, with professional lobbyists from the National
Education Association and the AFL-CIO, mobilized educational leaders from across the country. Nearly 900 educators were involved in meetings with their representatives
and with administration officials to try to override the president's veto. They came close but were unsuccessful by 52
votes.

Although the higher education associations were hesitant
about a full-fledged commitment to the emergency committee and did not have as much to gain or lose from participating in it as some of the other sectors of education did,
ACE sent a letter to several colleges and universities ask-
ing for money to support the committee, and that letter
was signed by executives from six other associations. A
small number of association officials and state office representatives did participate on the steering committee of the
emergency committee. But many association executives
were skeptical about participating or having higher education too closely allied with it. Some were put off by the
aggressive style of the lobbying effort. Some felt that
higher education was in danger of losing its long-sought-
after identification with the national interest as it participated in lobbying for a special interest.

An ACE official expressed the feelings of many higher
education association members:

> *I did have misgivings about crawling into bed with [so]
> many other interests like the labor unions and the impact
> aid people. . . . It's becoming increasingly difficult these
> days to convince Congress about the value of higher
> education to the nation and society through logical dis-
> cussion* (cited in King 1975, p. 70).

That the association community participated at all in the
emergency committee indicated that various ways of
increasing the role of associations in monitoring and influencing federal policy were going to continue.

The Sullivan report
The Association of American Colleges, as an association
comprised primarily of small, private, church-related insti-

tutions, had until the 1950s directly and adamantly opposed federal aid to higher education. In the 1950s, however, the association began to include in its membership a number of state teachers colleges that were being transformed into liberal arts institutions. Those institutions were not at all reluctant to receive federal aid, and by the late 1960s, over the resistance of a small group of Protestant colleges and independent colleges, the association began to favor federal aid to colleges and universities.

During the 1960s, AAC's leadership came to be firmly identified with ACE's published views on educational legislation. Because of the association's long history of representing private colleges and universities, its influx of public institutions, and its subsequent attempts to represent both groups by emphasizing its role as the representative of public and private liberal education, however, college presidents representing the independent liberal arts sector reacted intensely. They were vocal in asserting that AAC no longer represented independent education and that that entire sector had no voice and no representation among the associations in Washington.

The Sullivan report seems to have been an attempt to forestall the increase of exclusive, special interest voices operating in Washington that would divide the community. AAC President Richard H. Sullivan, in his 1969 annual report, proposed a system that would take into account the increasingly necessary, aggressive role that the higher education community needed to play in Washington. He wanted to make the community more directly a political entity but keep it as unified as possible. The private liberal arts colleges asked for stronger, more aggressive special representation in Washington.

Sullivan advocated the formation of two new associations in Washington: a lobbying organization and an information-generating and -distributing organization to explain higher education to the public (King 1975, p. 61). He thought the two organizations were necessary for two reasons. First, higher education was diverse and not well enough organized to obtain its goals. A new association devoted exclusively to lobbying would give higher education the kind of active political instrument it needed to have the desired effect on federal decision making. Second, Sullivan believed that people at the grass roots, both in and out of higher education, did not understand higher education. He thought the second organization was necessary to get "the American people to understand with more sophistication and realism the processes and institutions of higher education . . ." (King 1975, p. 62).

While neither the Emergency Committee for the Full Funding of Education nor the Sullivan report became the major means of increasing the association community's activities in federal relations, both affected the way in which the association community would operate in the future. Participation in the emergency committee became a normal part of the community's federal activities. (NAICU's formation in 1976 had as its exclusive purpose lobbying, not necessarily for the whole community but for the independent sector.) And a public relations group was organized to mobilize political efforts at the grass roots.

By the late 1960s, association community members could look back with some satisfaction upon what had been accomplished in Washington. In the face of some powerful divisive forces, a system had been erected that seemed to coordinate many aspects of higher education at the national level—relations with Congress and the executive branch, the gathering and distribution of information, and even provision for a national job market for administrators. The character of the 1970s began to emerge in the late 1960s, when the circumstances in which higher education and the associations were operating changed greatly.

During the 1960s, federal aid to support higher education advanced spectacularly. The major impediments that had been so controversial and prevented education laws from being passed—civil rights issues, church/state controversies, and fear of control by the federal government—had never been as significant for higher education as for the public schools, and, having been partially solved for the public schools through Title IV and other similar legislation, the 1960s passed in a climate favorable to higher education legislation.

The years from 1963 to 1968 were particularly prosperous for higher education, and income and expenditures for higher education rose even more rapidly than the expanding enrollment (Gladieux and Wolanin 1976, p. 20). But the era also saw widespread campus disruption that threatened to so alienate Congress and the voters that funds were in danger of being reduced or cut off for students and faculty involved in campus disorders.

By the late 1960s, institutions of higher education began to experience substantial financial trouble. A high rate of inflation, a slowing down of increases in federal spending for research, and reductions in financial assistance for graduate students led to large deficits in some schools, the actual demise of some institutions, and in general a change from thinking in terms of expansion of enrollments and faculties to the necessity to think in terms of reduction and reallocation. "The talk, the planning, and the decisions . . . center[ed] on reallocating, on adding only by substitution, or cutting, trimming and even struggling to hang on" (Cheit 1971, p. 3).

THE 1970s: THE NIXON-FORD-CARTER YEARS

When Richard Nixon became president in the 1970s, the place of higher education in American life was reappraised. Colleges and universities began to be seen as inefficient, expensive, wasteful, unwilling to change, and of doubtful benefit to the nation and to individuals (Gladieux and Wolanin 1976, p. 26). They were also viewed as housing and pampering radicals and malcontents. With all the difficulties that were perceived to be part of higher education, it was nevertheless clear to most people in higher education and government that the federal government's role in funding higher education was going to increase substantially.

As the 1970s began, the federal activities of the major associations increased considerably. Part of this increased activity was the result of the need of general higher education to respond to the impact of the legislation that had passed in the 1960s. But other serious and difficult financial problems had surfaced in higher education, particularly among the small, private, liberal arts colleges, and, with the fear of federal control through the acceptance of federal money attenuated, higher education looked to the federal government for help in relieving financial difficulties. For several years, the independent sector had been painting a picture of economic disaster in which it was predicted that many of the private institutions would not survive the next period without help. Some argued that only a few of the largest and wealthiest private institutions would remain (Gladieux and Wolanin 1978, p. 203).

As the 1970s began, the federal activities of the major associations increased considerably.

The Quest for Unity and the 1972 Higher Education Amendments

By 1970, the associations, led by ACE, were convinced that they must band together on as many issues as possible and speak with a united voice. Disunity had encouraged Congress to believe that higher education had no position on some issues that were vital to colleges and universities or that the higher education community was simply indecisive. Unity on policy did give the associations more persuasive strength, and when the associations agreed, they often succeeded in getting much of what they wanted.

Unity has its negative aspects as well, however. Some association representatives noted that the quest for unity in the early 1970s was so strong that the associations lost flexibility in their attempts to retain existing ties. Others thought that when efforts to build and maintain consensus were too avid, illuminating important issues and aspects of the associations' relationship to government and to students and institutions were buried.

The associations, so singularly dependent on the philosophy of a united front in some respects, were delighted that the major issue arising by the early 1970s was the question of institutional aid versus direct student aid. It was a good issue for several reasons. First, the associations welcomed the shift in decision making from those close to the president to Congress. In Congress they believed they had strong support for institutional aid in the person of Representative Edith Green, the head of the Special Subcommittee on Education, and important allies in Representatives Albert Quie and John Brademas. Further, the House of Representatives had expertise in higher education and had been the more active of the two branches of Congress. But the associations, particularly ACE, did not grasp the political dynamics operating inside the relevant subcommittee of the House or the position of Senator Claiborne Pell. Considerable infighting occurred. Representatives Quie and Brademas opposed Representative Green, and Senator Pell mistrusted the higher education community and became angry at the associations and their positions on the question of federal aid.

Most of the associations seemed not to understand that national opinion was going against them. While not opposing direct student aid, they continued to express more interest in institutional aid, even as large forces were lining up to prepare the way for a major change in public policy—a reallocation or redistribution of resources that would occur through direct student aid.

The issue reached a fever pitch when it came time to review the Higher Education Act of 1965 and its mandates. When the smoke had cleared and the 1972 Amendments had become law, the direction of federal aid to higher education was unmistakably through direct aid to students and not institutional aid. The associations had lost in a big way. Edith Green resigned her post on the education subcommittee and moved to the House Appropriations Committee. The associations were left with little that they had agreed they wanted. They were in great disarray, as their carefully orchestrated strategy of coalition building and speaking with one united voice had left people with the impression that the associations were out of touch with current thinking about higher education and that they cared more about unity in their public pronouncements than they did about responding to the needs of students and parents.

The debacle created the circumstances for considerable change in the community of associations and the way in which they did business. For the new president of ACE, Roger Heyns, it meant a relatively free hand, at least for a short time, to make changes that would build up the whole government relations area of ACE, to reorganize and appoint a new team, and to look for new solutions that would not rely too heavily upon total unity among the associations on any single issue. His mandate to bring about creative changes was enhanced by the Honey-Crowley report (1972), which strongly recommended changing the direction of ACE and increasing its political clout. In addition, Honey wrote a widely read, stinging attack on the associations in *Science* magazine, noting that the amendments would profoundly affect education for a long time and plainly asserting that the "failure of the Washington-based spokesmen for higher education to contribute significantly to the shaping of those amendments verges on the scandalous" (Honey 1972, p. 1243).

The 1972 Amendments and the role that the associations did not play in pushing them through created the conditions for a considerable amount of change in the associations. In passing the Higher Education Amendments of 1972, Congress produced the most significant higher education law of the 1970s. It set the tone for much of what followed in the decade and continues, even today, to be the legislative centerpiece that defines the terms in which many of the present federal government–higher education relationships and controversies are discussed and negotiated.

Government Regulations and Student Aid

A most significant section of the 1972 Amendments was the Basic Educational Opportunity Grants (BEOGs). This program extended and changed the federal commitment to equal opportunity in the 1965 act to a "direct entitlement" program that reflected the notion that qualified students would have access to higher education. It was clearly a decision that favored student aid over institutional aid and a statement of government responsibility for equal educational opportunity for all.

After the 1972 Amendments indicated the form and direction of a large portion of aid to higher education, another, not altogether new, issue became visible in the higher education–federal government arena—the onerous task of dealing with federal government regulations. It was an issue that preoccupied associations and higher education administrators for a major portion of the 1970s.

Government regulation was not new, but until the 1970s, most government regulation of institutions was at the state level. Regulation by the federal government was not an important source of irritation and conflict, even in the post–World War II period of the G.I. Bill and increased federal funding of research on college campuses. Although problems existed, they did not seem to cause the uproar that regulations did in the 1970s. In the 1960s, the main difficulties were not interference in the directions of and procedure for research but in the realization of a growing dependence upon the federal government for funds. This dependence later made the institutions susceptible to broadly ranging regulations (those related to affirmative action, for example), which were not intended solely for higher education but for all organizations receiving federal money. Further, some colleges and universities were affected by direct federal intervention to desegregate institutions of higher education.

The federal programs of the 1970s were more numerous and much more complex than those of the 1960s. New areas of governmental control—environmental laws, safety regulations, and antidiscrimination laws, for example—all required federal monitoring. The accountability of institutions to the federal government was increasingly stressed. The 1972 Amendments represented a widening of the areas of legitimate federal intrusion and regulation (Gladieux and Wolanin 1976, p. 39), and college and university presidents and administrators saw in the perceived increases of regulatory activity a future of rising administrative costs, time-consuming and irksome red tape, an attenuation of institutional control over academic affairs, and threats to academic freedom.

Presidents of colleges and universities became concerned about the regulations that had been accumulating since the 1960s and into the 1970s in the areas of social action—the Equal Pay Act of 1963, the Civil Rights Act of 1964, the Equal Employment Opportunity Act of 1964, Executive Order 11246 in 1965, the Age Discrimination in Employment Act of 1967, social security tax increases, the Occupational Safety and Health Act of 1970, Environmental Protection Agency regulations, aid to the handicapped, and the Family Educational Rights and Privacy Act of 1974. They all seemed to higher education administrators to weigh heavily on colleges and universities in the 1970s (Advisory Commission 1981).

The Distribution of Federal Funds and Institutional Problems

In the early 1970s, the financial problems of institutions of higher education were much on the minds of college presidents and the associations. An aura of financial crisis and alarm concerning the actual survival of colleges and universities was particularly notable in the private sector, and the issue was introduced into the legislative debates that preceded the Higher Education Amendments of 1972 (Gladieux and Wolanin 1976, p. 202).

Congress, however, did not respond to the dire predictions emanating from private colleges and universities, and it became quite apparent as the 1970s proceeded that the independent sector was not disappearing as predicted. Then private institutions developed the theme that the financial cutbacks and sacrifices necessary for survival were creating conditions that endangered their ability to retain their most prized assets—autonomy and uniqueness (Gladieux and Wolanin 1978, p. 203). They also perceived that the increasing differences in tuition between private and public institutions was a threat to the private schools' ability to retain and maintain a socioeconomically diverse student body. In fact, they argued, if the tuition differential continued to increase, the threat to the survival of private colleges and universities would return and accelerate.

Once the associations recognized and accepted that the federal government was going to provide financial aid to higher education primarily through the instrument of student aid, both public and private institutions concentrated on attempting to convince Congress and the succeeding administrations in Washington that such aid should be plentiful. The private institutions were particularly concerned that federal aid to students must take into consideration the growing and troublesome differences between private and public tuition and that the federal government should not place independent colleges and universities at such a disadvantage that they would be unable to compete for students. At the same time, public institutions were concerned that everyone be provided with enough aid to be able to go to school.

As the issue of student versus institutional aid faded into the background, federal aid to students emerged as the significant strategy pursued by Congress and by both the Nixon and Ford administrations. The general overall issue then became how the federal government was to distribute a finite amount of money that would improve education but not discriminate against either the public or the private schools. The question of how to promote equity, equality, and quality in higher education was to haunt higher education and the Washington higher education community for the rest of the decade and into the 1980s. (In 1984, the issue heated up to an incandescent point that threatened to undo, at least temporarily, the cooperation and information sharing that had been so carefully nurtured by the associations in the 1970s.) The problem was and is that despite the need and the will to treat private and public higher education evenhandedly, the aid system as it was constituted in the late 1970s and early 1980s had the consequence of treating the private and public sectors differently. An equitable formula acceptable to both sectors has so far eluded national decision makers.

The Haves and the Have Nots
A basis for increasingly difficult problems since the post–World War II period is the distinction between the "haves" and the "have nots" among colleges and universities. The distinction refers to a number of items—differences in size, resources, prestige, number of wealthy and generous alumni, endowments, capital resources, ability to recruit and retain attractive students and faculty, and so on. While the continuum from rich to poor is long and multidimensional with blurred gradations (and while all institu-

tions need additional funds), it is still evident that some institutions have more than others. No particular association includes only the haves as members, although the Association of American Universities comes close, and no association among the Big Seven includes only have nots, although the American Association of State Colleges and Universities and the Association of American Colleges represent fairly large numbers of institutions with somewhat thin resources.

The distinction between public and private control is not as important for the haves as it is for the have nots. The haves are most often heavily involved in graduate education and research and are likely to be united on such questions as aid to graduate students and what to do about government regulations on research and the level of funding for whom.

For the have nots, the differences between public and private institutions are exacerbated. The lifeblood of the publicly controlled have nots is low tuition and federal grants that cover a large percentage of total costs for a student, thus attracting students who might not otherwise attend college. For the private have nots, the necessity for federal funding based upon "need" rather than "across-the-board" financing is so great that, without something like the half-cost funding formula, many institutions believe they would go out of business altogether.

The following matrix illustrates the kinds of problems and positions that the Big Seven find themselves confronting on the basis of where they stand in the private/public dichotomy and the distinction between haves and have nots. When associations fit into all four categories, they can represent communitywide positions (like ACE) or a specialized interest (like AAC). Associations with members in all four categories tend to seek resolution of conflict within the association and within the community and attempt to formulate a unified approach to federal relations.

When associations are present in two of the four categories (like AAU), the controversy between private and public institutions is muted, but the differences between haves and have nots are increased. Even more significant, however, is the case of NAICU, which finds itself concerned but less involved in the differences between haves and have nots and a great deal more concerned about public/private controversies.

	Public	**Private**
Haves	ACE	ACE
	AAU	AAU
	NASULGC	NAICU
	AAC	AAC
Have Nots	AASCU	ACCU*
	CASC*	NAICU
	AACJC	CASC*
	ACE	AACJC
	AAC	ACE
		AAC
		CPCU*

*ACCU—Association of Catholic Colleges and Universities, CASC—Council for the Advancement of Small Colleges, CPCU—Council of Protestant Colleges and Universities.

When an association is represented in only one category (like AASCU), it often finds itself at odds with the entire private sector, both predominantly haves and predominantly have nots, and less than totally satisfied with even the association whose members are predominantly publicly controlled institutions (NASULGC) or with the associations whose members are a mix of public and private institutions (AAU and ACE). Because the public/private controversy strikes directly at the heart of institutional survival, the differences between public and private institutions are of the greatest significance to AASCU. The Protestant- and Catholic-affiliated college associations, although from the private sector, are in the same relative position as AASCU but count for less as individual associations than does AASCU. Thus, they find themselves most comfortable under NAICU's umbrella.

The Washington Education Associations Engage the 1970s
The basic thrust of the 1970s was to involve the federal government ever more deeply into higher education's affairs, and the individual associations and the community of associations could respond in no other way than to engage more actively and substantively in a relationship with the federal government. If it had not been clear to

everyone before 1972 that the most important business of most of the core associations was federal relations, there was little doubt about it later. (Although it was not, nor is it still, the area where most associations spend their energies and resources, it is nevertheless the most important.) Even so, the associations' activity in governmental relations was limited:

> *Obviously, the governmental relations of higher education are widely distributed and comprise only a part of the activities of the associations. It is estimated that about 35 people within the associations are devoting all of their time to federal relations, and about 24 are devoting half their time, for a total of about 50 full-time people* (Heyns 1973, p. 93).

In 1972, the associations faced not only a great deal of pressure to engage actively in federal relations to reenter the game after the events of 1972 but also a growing need to obtain more federal funds, to stave off increasingly irritating and bothersome government regulations, to reduce the rift between private and public institutions, and to mute the confrontations between the haves and have nots. These difficulties produced another dilemma: how to represent each segment of higher education and each institution more aggressively at the national level while coordinating the activities of the associations' diverse members.

The associations responded. ACE, which had borne the brunt of criticism in the late 1960s and early 1970s for failing to organize a strong higher education presence in Washington, could not realistically become an association able to satisfy all of its constituencies completely and at the same time aggressively pursue the cause of higher education in Washington. But, beginning in 1972, substantial changes improved its organizational and political structure and its machinery for quickly and effectively responding to the issues of national consequence to higher education.

Some of the most important changes took place in the Council itself. Roger Heyns, previously chancellor of the University of California–Berkeley, succeeded Logan Wilson as president of ACE. Heyns used much of his first year in office to try to understand how the association and the community operated, to deal with the Council's financial problems, and to develop the Council's priorities. He presented three general areas for work at the Council's annual meeting in 1972: to take the lead in developing a rationale for who should finance higher education by initiating new and improving existing planning and coordinating mechanisms (particularly with the Education Commission of the States); to take seriously and act upon the reports of the various commissions that had recently studied various aspects of higher education; and to consider such issues as institutional autonomy, the rights of women and minorities, and the maintenance of diversity in higher education (Semas 1972).

Although he planned to expand the budget of the Council's federal relations commission, Heyns saw federal relations as only one of a large number of activities in which the Council should be engaged. In his first years, Heyns took the important step of appointing Stephen K. Bailey as vice president of the Council, a position that had been vacant during the last years of Logan Wilson's tenure as president. Bailey was a well-known, highly respected political scientist from Syracuse University and was likely to appreciate the significance of increased activity in federal relations. With Bailey's aid, Heyns began reshaping the Council's federal relations program.

Another significant appointment was the recruitment of Charles B. Saunders to replace John Morse as director of ACE's Division of Governmental Relations. Saunders's Washington background was extensive: He had been a Senate staffer on educational issues, deputy assistant secretary of education, and acting assistant secretary of education during part of the Nixon administration.

Saunders began a series of internal changes that greatly enhanced the capacity of the Council and the Washington community to monitor and respond to activities on Capitol Hill and in the White House. He brought together an informal group in late 1974 that began to meet weekly. Its purpose was to act as a mechanism for regular interaction among the Big Six on governmental matters. It was later expanded to include several other associations, among them the National Association of College and University Business Officers and the National Association of Independent Colleges and Universities. Saunders's ambitious intent was to have the group share information, discuss issues with which the community should be dealing, talk about how the issues should be dealt with, and then divide the responsibility for dealing with the issues.

In an effort to have the ACE Division of Governmental Relations increase its role as coordinator, Saunders's office and Saunders himself began drafting position papers on federal issues expressing the associations' sense of the issues and their position or positions on them. The division circulates drafts of these position papers to the community of associations and seeks comments from their executive officers. Given enough consensus, the associations approve the drafts; sometimes the issue concerns only a few associations, so only those affected approve it; and occasionally, divisions among the various associations are so deep that ACE and the Division of Governmental Relations must back off and find a new position.*

Later, Saunders began conducting a weekly meeting of a much larger group (35 to 40) of association representatives, including some from the National Education Association and student associations. This group essentially acts as a monitor; it meets every Friday and participants talk about upcoming issues and what happened the previous week.

The capability for policy analysis for the Washington association community had been talked about for years and recommended in 1971 (Bloland and Wilson 1971), but nothing was implemented until the Council inaugurated the Policy Analysis Service in the summer of 1973. Its tasks included studying policy issues, gathering and arranging data on issues, preparing summaries of policy issues, and responding to queries from Congress and the president (McNamara 1976a). From the beginning, the Policy Analysis Service was engaged in what became its primary task, providing support services to ACE's Division of Governmental Relations (Heyns 1977, p. 1).

The Honey-Crowley report, referred to earlier, called for drastic changes in the organization of the Council, among them a number of recommendations directed toward a much heavier concentration in government relations. President Heyns accepted these recommendations only in part; he was opposed to the idea ''that the Council be exclusively (or nearly so) concerned with governmental rela-

Saunders began a series of internal changes that greatly enhanced the capacity of the Council and the Washington education community. . . .

*Charles B. Saunders 1984, interview.

tions" (King 1975, p. 102). But he was concerned with the service role of the Council. Programs and services like Academic Affairs, Women in Higher Education, Administrative Affairs, and Leadership Development have been important in creating and sustaining ACE's image in the higher education world. More important, they have helped generate funds for the services and other activities needed to carry on the Council's role. This service role, however, was to have its own negative consequences in ACE's relations with other associations.

Heyns also has a strong sense of the political limitations of the Council in the Washington community. Its membership covers the entire range of educational interests, and many of them are incompatible. Other associations that are members of the Council have their own agendas and their own constituents. The community is, after all, a group of autonomous associations whose cooperation with one another is always voluntary. The Council realistically had to approach a more active role somewhat slowly, however impatient its critics. Heyns stressed the cooperative role of ACE, not its activist role. He strongly urged that the position of the Council as "coordinator, convener, and catalyst" be emphasized, terms that have come up again and again in discussions of the Council's role (Heyns 1977, p. 6). "The basic posture has been for the Council to encourage joint efforts, to avoid duplication, and to limit its own efforts to those problems that are of concern to the entire postsecondary community" (p. 6).

To implement this posture, Heyns developed the concept of the "lead agency" or the "chosen instrument":

The associations should collectively agree that, whenever appropriate, one association will be responsible for discharging a particular function. The implications are that no one else will duplicate that function, and all will help the chosen instrument (Heyns 1973, p. 94).

The concept of chosen instrument was used as a method to deal partially with the overlap and duplication that had been plaguing the educational associations for some years.

Internally, other innovations occurred in the Council's structure and activities during Heyns's tenure of office. A particularly strong criticism of the Council had been its relationship with member associations—the group of associations that had been instrumental in creating the Council in 1918. Those groups had felt for years that the Council's policies should reflect their concerns, if not totally, at least substantially. And the way to accomplish that aim was to have more direct representation on the Council's major decision-making bodies. In 1973, this change was partially effected by a constitutional change that added representatives from the associations to the Council's Board of Directors. The association representatives to the board were the university and college presidents who had been elected heads of their respective associations.

Further, in 1973, a body consisting of those presidents elected as heads of the major associations (that is, the elected head of the American Council on Education and the elected heads and the "hired hand" executive heads of the other Big Six associations) was introduced. Informally called the Coordinating Committee, the group was later expanded to include the elected head and the executive head of the National Association of Independent Colleges and Universities. The committee's task was to enhance the coordinating function of the association community by identifying issues and problems requiring cooperation and to help choose and monitor the lead agencies that would concentrate on the problems (Heyns 1977, p. 4). This approach did not work well, for, according to one top association official, "the people who knew everything were the hired hands, so the presidents just sat back and listened. And the hired hands talked in front of their principals. Instead of the principals' calming the bureaucrats down and saying, 'Hey fellows, get together,' what happened was each one was showing his principal what a genius he was." This committee also suffered from growth pangs. Everyone wanted to be a member, and the bigger it became, the less effective it was.

Also under Heyns's leadership, the Secretariat was reconstituted as a formal part of the Council's organizational structure. Even though the president of the Council had presided over its meetings since its inception, the Secretariat was always an independent body of association executives. The Secretariat continued its role as an arena for information exchange and as an informal coordinating instrument, but under Heyns's leadership, the ACE president became more formally responsible for its work, and ACE provided support staff for the implementation of its activities. The Secretariat also began to increase in size and, in doing so, reduced its role as a decision-making organization while retaining its function as an important forum for the exchange of ideas.

Perhaps the most important consequence of the formalization and growth of the Secretariat was the president's decision to form a smaller, informal group of the executive heads of seven major presidentially based associations. This group came to be known as "The Brethren," and it became the most important body to identify and debate higher education, exchange information, and coordinate policy in the higher education community.

Community Changes and Activities
The public sector

Although all of the associations were changing and adjusting to the modified circumstances of the 1970s, in many ways, NASULGC, AASCU, and AACJC kept a steady course by participating in the community, responding to their constituents' needs, and presenting the case for public institutions in higher education. In some areas, however, differences among these three associations surfaced as controversies from time to time. Although interested in undergraduate education, NASULGC was at the forefront in representing the interests of graduate education (with AAU and ACE), particularly in research and in generating research money from the federal government. NASULGC opposed the increase of federal regulation that accompanied those research funds. These issues were of less significance to AASCU but at times caused real consternation among the institutional members of AACJC. It sometimes appeared to AACJC that a piece of legislation or a regulation favored graduate education and/or research at the expense of undergraduate education, particularly in two-year colleges.

In the 1970s, other changes in the individual associations not only affected those associations but also modified the community of associations by changing their internal community relationships and their relationships with government.

The Association of American Universities

AAU had maintained a publicly passive posture toward the federal government and other associations well into the late 1960s. Even the increased flow of federal funds to AAU members did not make the association activist in the early and mid-1960s. By 1967 and 1968, however, the combination of turmoil on their campuses and the slowdown in the increase of federal support for research led the AAU's leaders to create a formal organizational structure for dealing with the federal government—the Council on Federal Relations. Dr. Charles Kidd, a career government official with considerable experience and expertise accumulated from service in the Federal Council on Science and Technology, the Social Security Administration, the Council of Economic Advisors, and the National Institutes of Health, was named director of the AAU's Council on Federal Relations in 1969. He became executive secretary of the association in 1971. AAU was launched on a more active program of federal relations.

In the mid to late 1970s, the AAU leadership again consciously decided to upgrade the level of its activities to become a more aggressive association in relation to the federal government and to increase its staff. It continued to work closely with the other associations, particularly with NASULGC and ACE.

The politicization of the independents: From AAC to NAICU

Among the most dramatic changes in the Washington higher education community were those affecting AAC. For most of its existence, AAC had been one of the most conservative of the core associations and, as late as 1963, had opposed any federal aid to institutions of higher education. The major opposition to the association's involvement with the federal government had been from a small group of presidents of Protestant-affiliated colleges. In 1962, for example, during critical House Rules Committee deliberations on the Higher Education Facilities Act, they sent telegrams to the committee opposing federally sponsored aid for construction and scholarships and testified in a Senate committee against the bill, against federal aid in general, and in support of tax credits (King 1975, p. 68). This stance had considerable effect on AAC as a whole and contributed greatly to its conservative image of eschewing involvement with the federal government. This antipolitical stance changed considerably in 1967, however, when more than 100 representatives of colleges and associations from the private sector assembled in Washington to discuss means for establishing effective national representation for the independent colleges and universities, a necessary representation they felt was lacking at the time. This movement represented several strains of thought in the independent sector of higher education. One was expressed by President Weimer Hicks of Kalamazoo College:

> *Most of us connected with small colleges are anti federal legislation. . . . But if the game is going to be played with Washington as the focal point, then we have to be in Washington* (cited in King 1975, p. 87).

More important for the community and for AAC, however, was that the deep division within AAC was brought to public attention. From its beginnings, AAC had provided a home and representation for liberal arts schools and the liberal arts perspective. Thus, AAC included and reflected the interests of not just the small independent colleges but also public institutions and large institutions whose interests were in liberal education, indicated by the inclusion of a number of liberal arts deans from large institutions.

The presidents of small, independent colleges looked around and saw that the other sectors of higher education each were strongly represented in Washington. None of the associations seemed dedicated to the specific interests of the small, independent colleges, particularly when it seemed to representatives of those institutions that the public institutions were getting a continually larger share of the nation's students, money, and other resources.

By the late 1960s, AAC had been deeply involved in the problems of undergraduate institutions in relation to the federal government. Also during the 1960s, the Federation of State Associations of Independent Colleges and Universities (FSAICU) had been formalized as a national coordinating agency for the independent schools within AAC, and AAC provided it with staff, funds, and space. It had its own board of directors and executive secretary. In continuing to pursue a more active policy for independent colleges and universities, FSAICU was reorganized in 1971, becoming the National Council for Independent Colleges and Universities (NCICU). To further its interests in federal relations, it named Howard Holcomb as director of federal affairs (Hunt 1977, p. 50). Now its board presumably could stake its own position in federal affairs, completely independent from AAC. NCICU was still part of AAC, however, which continued to supply staff and funds for its activities.

In 1975, a study undertaken by Edgar Carlson, executive director of the Minnesota Private College Council, concluded that "there must be a separate national voice for the independent sector" (Hunt 1977, p. 51). AAC, if it wished to take this study seriously, could eliminate its public school members or establish an organization separate from AAC to represent the independent sector of higher education. Carlson favored creating a new organization, and the plan was approved at an AAC/NCICU meeting.

A new independent organization, the National Association of Independent Colleges and Universities, was formed, and NCICU was disbanded. This move left AAC free to pursue its interests in liberal education and the new organization to represent private colleges and universities. NAICU became an association with a diverse membership that included not only large, established, independent research universities but also, according to its brochure, "two-year colleges and technical institutes; four-year liberal arts colleges—some nonsectarian, others church- or faith-related; schools of business, music, bible study, theology, health, and law."*

NAICU quickly became the seventh member of the Big Six and a core association with satellite associations around it. It became an umbrella association for the independent sector with an umbrella association's problems.

I feel as though I'm trying to manage a very complicated kind of rickety umbrella, with some of the spokes being longer and shorter and lots of tilting and winds threatening to turn the umbrella completely inside out.†

*NAICU brochure 1983, p. 1.
†John Phillips 1984, interview.

As an umbrella organization with diverse members displaying diverse interests, its problem became similar to some of those of ACE. Almost 90 percent of NAICU's potential members had fewer than 2,500 students, but the NAICU board of directors started with the presidents of Johns Hopkins, Stanford, and Boston universities on it. The question of domination by big schools was raised early in NAICU's history (Hunt 1977, p. 51) but was later muted. And, as if to punctuate its umbrella status, NAICU organized a group of association executive directors and called it the Secretariat, in the fashion of ACE and its Secretariat.

During the transitional and somewhat hectic mid-1970s, the private sector spawned other organizations intended to pinpoint specific interests of the independent sector while representing the whole of the private college spectrum. They were invariably viewed as reflecting not the whole private sector but some segment of it. Such an association was the Consortium on Financing of Higher Education (COFHE). Formed in 1974, its 30 member institutions were characterized as private, elite, and prestigious. Its purpose was to serve its members through planning, research, and consulting. Its initial chair was David Truman, president of Mount Holyoke College, and although its headquarters were not in Washington, it was represented in Washington. COFHE published an influential report on federal aid to students in 1975. Well-researched and -written, the report recommended modifying basic and supplemental grant programs to students in ways COFHE hoped the private sector would approve and the public sector would not oppose. Much of the independent sector did not view the recommendations positively, however, and only AAU and ACE gave it even limited support (Gladieux and Wolanin 1978, p. 211). Its major drawback, as far as the small colleges were concerned, was its proposal to eliminate the half-cost limit on student aid at a time when the small colleges were strongly attached to it in principle. The report also proposed that what was gained by increase in access could be made up by including supplementary grants tied loosely to tuition costs in private institutions. It was not clear to many schools that this proposal would benefit small private institutions, and some risk seemed to be involved in this change at a time when the private institutions feared that any change would jeopardize their existence. The small private colleges felt the proposal would benefit only large private institutions with higher tuition.

Student associations
Student associations had been quite active (aggressive but not sophisticated) in the late 1960s and early 1970s. The National Student Lobby was noted for its strong representation of students' consumer interests. The National Student Education Fund had been effective through its research and attempts to lead students' opinions (Hamilton 1977, p. 43). The National Student Association was not active in the passage of the 1976 Amendments to the Higher Education Act, but a new student organization representing students from private, prestigious schools—the Coalition of Independent University Students (COIUS)—became active.

In recent years, however, old Washington hands have not seen much activity from student associations and regard them as minor players in the Washington higher education scene. Activity among student associations apparently depends upon who is elected to the leadership.

By 1977, the associations were attempting "to anticipate and take the initiative on emerging issues. . . ."

The Improving Image: The Big Six in the 1970s
The 1976 Education Amendments, reauthorizing the 1972 Amendments, did not provoke the kind of heated controversy that was part of the legislative battles of 1972. The 1976 legislation consisted primarily of extensions of the 1972 act, and although some of the issues of 1972 re-emerged, the legislation did not change significantly.

By 1976, the image of the associations had changed. The blasts of the Honey-Crowley report, the harsh words of Senator Pell and Congressman Brademas, the negative position of Senator Moynihan, and the bleak picture painted by Gladieux and Wolanin gave way to a more optimistic view of the associations. The wallflower began to dance, and Senator Pell found the higher education associations more helpful in his efforts to extend and amend the 1972 Amendments (McNamara 1976b). The associations made progress, becoming "effective voices in the formulation of federal higher education policy" (Wolanin 1976, p. 184). By 1977, the associations were attempting "to anticipate and take the initiative on emerging issues rather than reacting to and having to catch up with events" (Gladieux

1977, p. 43). This optimism, however, was tempered by reminders of how far the associations had to go to be really effective, particularly in lobbying the grass roots, but generally the associations received considerably higher marks by the mid-1970s.

The Council's new president: Jack Peltason

In the spring of 1977, to the surprise of the Washington association community, Roger Heyns announced his intention to resign as president of ACE. Jack Peltason, chancellor of the Champaign/Urbana campus of the University of Illinois, was selected as the eighth president of the American Council on Education. Peltason, a political scientist, took office in the fall of 1977. As with his predecessor, there was little doubt that change would occur during Peltason's tenure.

President Peltason continued ACE's development in the direction of a more sophisticated and knowledgeable agency in its relationship with the federal government and continued the search for ways to unite the higher education community on significant policy questions. He saw part of his mandate as broadening the areas of interest the Council would be involved in and increasing services to members.

Among Peltason's early acts was naming seven task forces to evaluate ACE and look at its future (Peltason 1978). The designation of the task forces indicated Peltason's perceptions of the Council's possibilities and limitations, and he invoked the now time-honored "coordination, convening, and catalytic" roles (Heyns 1973) as the essence of ACE's service to its constituency, stressing that ACE's responsibilities were large, its activities and their effects often invisible, its resources limited, and its staff small. Therefore, Peltason indicated, the Council needed to call upon the other Washington associations and their resources to "leverage" the capacity of the ACE staff (Peltason 1978, p. 2). More controversial was Peltason's proposal that modest "staff resources must be augmented more and more by ACE program money, venture capital, which we shall make strenuous efforts to raise" (p. 2).

Predictably, the first priority was to strengthen the Council's and other associations' influence on federal policies affecting higher education. Added to that priority was a commitment to enter the state government–higher education arena, initially by building the capacity to provide information on interrelated federal and state higher education policies. Peltason's second priority was to have the Council engage in more research directed toward issue-centered policy analysis, and the third was to broaden ACE's commitment to programs of continuing education for administrators and to identify and help place high-quality leaders in higher education, emphasizing the inclusion of women and minorities. Finally, ACE was to extend its efforts to increase communication with leaders from business, labor, and agriculture (Peltason 1978).

Change in the Council
Implementing these priorities meant recommending a reorganization of the Council. The first major change was aimed at improving the Council's coordinating function among the associations by allocating "permanent" places on ACE's board for the major institutionally based associations belonging to ACE.

The Division of Governmental Relations kept its central functions of coordinating and monitoring federal relations and its claim to first priority on policy research and results, but a state government relations section was added to the division, and Charles Saunders, director of the division, was named Vice President for Governmental Affairs. Thus, the way was clear for government relations to become an even more significant activity for ACE.

Peltason proposed to house most of the Council's programmatic functions, the direct services to the institutions, in the Division of Institutional Relations. The Division of Policy Analysis was placed under the leadership of Vice President Atwell and included policy analysis, economic and financial research, the higher education panel, and administrative and management issues. A Division of External Relations was proposed whose purpose would be to focus on public information (maintaining the library), membership development, and liaison with business, labor, and other groups. A Division of International Educational Relations would take under its jurisdiction many of the Council's international activities, leaving the Fulbright program an independent project.

Tax Credits and the Middle Income Student Assistance Act of 1978

With inflation rapidly driving the cost of education upward, considerable support was building in Congress for tax relief to middle-income families paying the expenses of their offspring in colleges and universities. The Senate was especially favorable to such legislation and had passed two such proposals in 1976.

Although those proposals failed to clear the House, the idea did not die, and in 1978, a tax relief proposal for middle-income families with children in college almost passed. The most formidable version was sponsored by Senators Packwood and Moynihan. Essentially, the bill would have allowed a tax credit of up to $100 in 1978 to be applied to a family's personal income tax. The maximum would be increased to $250 in 1979 (Advisory Commission 1981, p. 48). Such antagonists as the Carter administration, the American Federation of Teachers, the National Education Association, and *The Washington Post* strongly opposed the bill (McNamara 1978, p. 44).

The higher education associations were ambivalent about such legislation in 1978, primarily because it raised the possibility of benefiting the private more than the public sector. Even more important, the higher education associations were perhaps beginning to believe that direct infusions of money to all of higher education were a more necessary form of relief than tax credits.

The associations developed a plan for targeting additional aid to middle-income families through increases in the existing student aid programs. As of February 1, 1978, "virtually all of the major postsecondary education groups [had] signed off on a $2 billion student assistance package to be proposed as an alternative for tuition tax credits."* A week later Congressman William Ford introduced the Middle Income Student Assistance Act, which not only broadened eligibility for guaranteed student loans to all students but also raised the eligibility limits for Pell grants from $15,000 in family income to $25,000. Ford presented this bill as an alternative to tuition tax credits and used it to help persuade the somewhat reluctant Carter administra-

*Thomas Wolanin 1978, memorandum to Congressman Ford.

tion to sponsor the bill. The associations continued their heavy involvement in the legislation, participating in hearings and otherwise demonstrating their support for the bill from its inception to its passage. The legislation was passed in 1978.

The Department of Education

That education should have a stronger voice and more visible place in the federal government through its elevation to cabinet status had been part of the thinking of educators and administrators for many years, particularly among the leaders of elementary and secondary education. Jimmy Carter had expressed interest in the creation of a Department of Education in his 1976 presidential campaign, and the National Education Association (NEA) eagerly endorsed Carter for president soon after. The American Federation of Teachers opposed it, however, and the higher education community was unenthusiastic or ambivalent about the creation of such a department. Responding to the division within the ranks of higher education, ACE did not officially take a position on the issue (Advisory Commission 1981). President Peltason expressed some of the ambiguities of the higher education community in noting ". . . the fears are of greater regulation, and the hopes are that the department will be a platform of greater visibility" (p. 49).

The initial lack of enthusiasm on the part of higher education stemmed from several perceptions. It looked as though elementary and secondary education interests would dominate the department because of NEA's part in bringing about its creation and because budgets for elementary and secondary education federal programs were so large in comparison to those of higher education. Further, many astute observers of higher education relations have maintained for years that the dispersal of higher education programs to a variety of departments and bureaus has worked to the advantage of universities and colleges in many cases. The creation of a Department of Education might therefore lead to an unwelcomed consolidation of programs under the aegis of an unfriendly federal government unit.

In the later stages of the bill, however, the higher education community did find common ground upon which to support the formation of the Department of Education. While NEA had a major stake in the creation of the department and thus was perhaps less critical of the way in which programs were included or excluded, the higher education associations, led by ACE, expressed their reservations and pressed for specific changes that would attenuate their concerns. They advocated line responsibilities instead of staff positions for the assistant secretaries, opposed the transfer of the National Foundation on the Arts and Humanities to the new department, and supported the transfer of the College Housing Loan Program from the Department of Housing and Urban Development to the Education Department (Saunders 1978). The final version of the bill reflected most of their recommendations.

The Higher Education Reauthorization Act of 1980

In early fall 1980, Congress passed a landmark piece of legislation, the Education Amendments of 1980, extending federal higher education programs through fiscal year 1984–85. Recognizing that the costs of attending college had become much greater, Congress significantly raised the limits of federally financed grants and loans for students over the ensuing five years. Included in the act's benefits were raises in maximum Supplemental Educational Opportunity Grants, increases in State Student Incentive Grants, increases in dollars for the College Work Study programs, raises in the cumulative loan limits for both financially dependent and independent students, and a new low interest loan program for parents of dependent students. The act further provided for aid to urban universities and graduate fellowships. These provisions of the 1980 Amendments reflected most of the priorities expressed by spokesmen for higher education in Washington.

None of these provisions were as politically significant for the higher education community, however, as the provisions of the Basic Educational Opportunity Grants (BEOGs). Public institutions had been displeased with the previous legislation, which provided that education costs covered by federal grants could not be above 50 percent of a student's total costs. The consequence of that provision, the public institutions argued, was that a major burden was placed on less affluent students, who would have difficulty raising the other 50 percent of their total educational costs.

Thus, the public institutions, led by AASCU, called for changing the formula from 50 percent to a higher percentage. The private institutions favored retaining the half-cost rule and saw an increased percentage covered by federal grants as quite likely to encourage the movement of students from private institutions to public institutions, a drain perceived as threatening to the very existence of independent colleges and universities.

This conflict between public and private institutions had been plaguing the association community for some time, and the associations took steps to try to resolve the conflict reasonably before the reauthorization bill came up. The associations, with ACE as leader, over two and one-half years explored the dimensions of this and other legislative issues that divided the community and were likely to become major problems. They tried to foresee the implications of various alternative legislative options.

After much effort, the Washington associations and their members reached an understanding of the consequences for their organizations, individually and collectively, of the most likely decisions that would be made concerning the 1980 reauthorization bill. In the summer of 1979, Congressman Ford, chair of the Subcommittee on Postsecondary Education, challenged the association community to submit proposals for changes in the bill that they could agree upon as necessary and desirable.

By then, much preliminary work had been done, and the associations were able to agree on those proposals. After some intense consultation, the associations provided language for the legislation that spelled out precisely the extent of their agreement on a wide variety of proposals, particularly their agreement on BEOGs, the program that had been so troublesome for so long. Six association senior officials signed a letter to Congressman Ford spelling out the specific language agreed upon as a solution to the conflict over the half-cost provisions. The letter stated in part, "We believe this proposal provides a simple and straightforward method of alleviating the problems [that] have been associated with the half-cost limitation" (U.S. Congress 1979, p. 19).

The bill that emerged from the House Education and Labor Committee included most of the changes the community had proposed (ACE 1979a, p. 2). "Mr. Ford and the Subcommittee relied on the 'best' of what each of the students, university administrators, governmental officials, and legislators had to offer" *(Chronicle of Higher Education* 17 September 1979, p. 15).

The BEOG program that eventually passed raised the limit from $1,800 to $1,900 the first year, with increases in each of the following years to 1985–86, when the maximum was to reach $2,600. At the same time, the grants were limited in 1981–82 to 50 percent of an individual student's total costs, but thereafter the ceiling was raised by 5 percent each year to 1985–86, when it would reach 70 percent.

The two years of work culminating in the enactment of the law reflected the positive changes in the way the higher education community conducted its federal relations and in the improved image that law makers and congressional staff had of the associations and their ability to provide expert, correct, timely, and helpful information. From Senator Pell's reference to the associations as "the fudge factory in Dupont Circle" (Baker and Barnes 1980) to the favorable reviews from Capitol Hill in 1980 was a considerable and welcome distance for the associations.

End of the 1970s: Internal Turmoil and Solving Problems
As the end of the decade approached, some issues had been partially resolved, old issues had resurfaced, and new problems and possibilities were emerging.

The strong, hostile representations by university presidents against the perceived tide of federal regulations gave way to a sense that Congress was sympathetic and increasingly aware of the negative aspects of those regulations and was open to easing the burden they placed on institutions (Bailey 1978). Senator Pell, for example, in response to a speech by President Kingman Brewster of Yale attacking regulation by the federal government, stated for the *Congressional Record* that:

> *President Brewster's remarks are cogent. . . . He pointed out that there is a growing amount of control, not through direct intervention, but through oblique approaches. . . . Although his speech attacks some of the programs and bills which I have supported, I think his remarks should be read by every Senator* (Advisory Commission 1981, p. 44).

Although the Reauthorization Act of 1980 was not all that everyone in higher education could wish for and some deep divisions among the sectors were still not resolved, the associations had achieved major success in building community consensus and in setting in motion a collective course of action that was politically realistic and advantageous to the cause of higher education. In the late 1970s, however, one of those substantive, structural problems that the associations continually monitor, tinker with intermittently, and never quite resolve came to the fore once again. At its most basic level, it has to do with the associations' function of representation and how it should be done. In the form that it took in the late 1970s and early 1980s, it revolved around several direct questions and reached Dupont Circle from a variety of sources.

Institutions of higher education need national representation and the services that the Washington associations provide. But this representation, however much needed, tends to generate problems on occasion because at least three kinds of representation and three types of associations are involved. First, institutions need representation that speaks for the whole of higher education, the unified voice of higher education (ACE). Second, each sector (public, private, community colleges, and so on) needs its voice to be heard and to be counted in national decision making. Third, each institution includes units requiring a national voice (graduate schools, business officers, development people, and so on), each of which forms an association comprised of universities and colleges as members.

This picture is complicated immensely by the fact that some associations attempt to perform all three kinds of representation (the American Council on Education, for example), some try to represent the second and third (the American Association of State Colleges and Universities), and some tend to concentrate on one (the National Association of Independent Colleges and Universities). Adding to the whole ambiguous and messy situation is the fact that some associations (like ACE) perform both representation and service for their members and some only representation.

This multivoiced system of representation means that for an institution to be sufficiently represented in Washington, it may need to belong to a number of associations simultaneously and to pay dues to each. A large, research-oriented Class I university dominated by its graduate program, for example, might belong to ACE, NASULGC, AAC, the Council of Graduate Schools, the National Association of College and University Business Officers, and the Council for the Advancement and Support of Education. And this list is probably incomplete. Each association has annual dues, and in some cases fees are required for services. The dues can be substantial. In 1980, AAU's annual dues were a flat $13,000, ACE's ranged from $385 to $5,680, and AACJC's ranged from $500 to $1,500 (Scully 1979, p. 10).

If one institution pays dues for seven or eight memberships or more, the total cost can be great. When costs are cut back or budgets generally tightened, questions are raised: "Does the institution need to belong to all those associations?" "Is this membership in multiple organizations cost effective?" "Is it possible that several associations are supplying essentially the same representation and/or services?" And the final, ominous one, "Are we paying for unnecessary overlap and duplication?"

At that point, a call is often sounded for a study of the role of associations in Washington and their relationships with their members and with each other. In the late 1970s, the questions were serious enough to initiate two studies, one by an initial group of six presidents (the "Gang of Six," which eventually became identified as the "Gang of Ten") and the other by the faculty members of the higher education center of the University of Michigan under the direction of Dr. Joseph Cosand. A good deal of *sturm und drang* accompanied this examination of the associations' role because such study brings to the surface and accentuates the difficulties of dealing with a set of closely related and unresolved community problems.

First, what should be the role of the American Council on Education? Is it primarily an association of associations with a strictly coordinative role? Or is it, like other associations, an organization representing a constituency of institutions and therefore a rival of the other associations? This problem was exacerbated in the period before the two studies by the Council's decision to initiate new services in areas where other associations were already involved. ACE had organized a presidents committee on intercollegiate athletics and a council of chief academic officers within the Council, and other associations viewed it as invasions of their territory. This move played a part in originating the Gang of Six (Scully 1979, p. 10).

President Peltason's tenure had been marked by considerable action on the part of ACE. He reorganized, moved the Council into new fields, expanded its role, and generally maintained a strong presidency. He responded forcefully to the heat generated by ACE's initiatives:

Some people . . . think that the associations ought to be doing more together, rather than as individual segments. I've made it no secret that my mandate here is not just to add up what everybody thinks, but to be a catalyst and coordinator (Scully 1979, p. 10).

Although the Gang of Six seems to have originated as an independent band of dissident presidents of higher education institutions and executive heads of associations, it was domesticated quickly by an ACE board of directors meeting at the end of June 1979. The board decided that ACE's coordinating committee would sponsor a study and would seek funds to underwrite it (Fretwell 1980). Later, the coordinating committee instructed President Peltason to appoint a subcommittee to do the study (which included the original six presidents), and the study was underway.

The study had three major goals: (1) to study and make recommendations on the relations among the associations as presently structured; (2) to examine the "proliferation of specialized associations" (Fretwell 1980, p. 2); and (3) to look at other ways of organizing the national representation of higher education. The study concentrated on the first issue, but all three areas included other recommendations.

The Gang of Ten benefited from the Michigan study, *Presidential Views of Higher Education's National Institutional Membership Associations* (Cosand et al. 1980), which surveyed 1,284 presidents of colleges and universities and interviewed 33 knowledgeable observers of the national higher education scene. The subcommittee especially noted the finding of the Cosand study that more than one-third of the presidents, with a choice of five models of association relationships to choose from, favored the model of the *current, pluralistic* system, and another 27 percent chose the *stronger, coordinated* model.

In the Michigan study, the presidents generally viewed positively the associations to which their institutions belonged and saw federal relations as the central activity of ACE and the other associations for the 1980s (Cosand et al. 1980, p. 6). They saw the need for increased coordination of the associations to fulfill this mandate, but their view was tempered by the majority opinion among ACE members that members are not represented equally in the associations.

The responses of the 33 national observers in the Michigan study emphasized that the associations were "reactive to issues and problems" to a greater degree than were the presidents and stressed the value of a "unified position on important issues" (Cosand et al. 1980, p. 4).

After considering a variety of alternative structural models for the Council, the Gang of Ten rejected proposals to radically reorient the Council to resemble the organization of the AFL-CIO or the Chamber of Commerce (Fretwell 1981).

The report touched upon a number of aspects of association activities and relationships, including a call for more coordination, which was the Council's responsibility, an admonition to resolve the occupancy problems of One Dupont Circle and enhance its role as a National Center for Higher Education, a plea for a moratorium on new association programs and upon the creation of new associations, and a reminder that associations should remember the concept of "lead agency." The most important results of the subcommittee's findings were recommendations that the vice president of ACE be responsible for improving association relations and that associations check with each other before instituting new activities and policies that would affect other associations. This latter point was made prominently enough so that the Gang of Ten study became known as the "No Surprises Report."

THE 1980s: CONFRONTING THE REAGAN ADMINISTRATION

The National Elections of 1980 and Their Aftermath

The election of Ronald Reagan to the presidency and the sweeping changes that took place in Congress left the higher education community in a state of uncertainty and confusion. Although President Carter's search for "coherence and a sense of direction" had generally resulted in tighter restrictions on spending for higher education, significant legislation had passed in the Carter years—the 1976 Amendments to the Higher Education Act, the 1978 Middle Income Student Assistance Act, the 1980 Amendments, which raised the maximum benefits among higher education programs, and the law creating the Department of Education.

A major anchor for the education community in the Carter and previous administrations was the long-standing predictability of the ideological position that was reflected in the actions of Congress and the presidents. What Chester Finn characterized as "the liberal consensus" had developed and shaped national educational policy for more than 20 years (Finn 1980).

This liberal consensus envisioned a vigorous and active role for the federal government to achieve the goals of equal opportunity, access to schools, desegregation, encouragement and support for research, and elimination of discrimination involving age, sex, and race. "Reform and innovation" were emphasized (Wilson 1982, p. 10). And the federal government could be counted upon to use funding incentives and federal laws and regulations to achieve those ends.

> *The consensus sought to attenuate the exclusionary connection between a high level of income and access to education and to give more people a chance at educational opportunity than would have been the case if the federal government had kept out of the field* (Chester E. Finn, Jr., cited in Wilson 1982, p. 10).

The keepers of the liberal consensus were identified with a wide variety of institutions and organizations: the Ford Foundation and others, research-oriented universities, national associations (including many of those in the Big Six plus One), some members of Congress and the administration, newspapers like the *New York Times* and *The*

Washington Post, think tanks like the Brookings Institution, and influential individuals from higher education (Clark Kerr, Harold Howe, and Ernest Boyer) (Wilson 1982, pp. 9–10).

The amalgam of positions and policies among the liberal consensus was viewed positively—or at least neutrally— by many different groups, particularly in education. As the 1980 elections drew near, however, the long-standing issue of the balance between equality and quality in education became more acute and threatened the stability of the liberal consensus in Washington. How educational policies should be shaped by emphasis upon one or the other and how funds should be distributed in relation to quality and equality were issues brought to public attention by budget problems, inflation, questions of accountability, student achievement, regulations, and ambivalence about affirmative action. The debate was considerably enlivened by the challenge to the liberal consensus posed by a neoconservative position whose most articulate representatives were closely connected with the academic world—Sidney Hook, Nathan Glazer, and Peter Drucker, for example.

The Reagan Presidency
As the 1980 elections approached, the education community was not certain about what would happen to existing higher education programs, but events strongly indicated cutbacks in educational funding and programs. The Reagan campaign had stressed an attack on inflation, reduction of taxes and government regulation, control of the federal deficit, and concentration on national defense. The rhetoric of the campaign indicated considerable hostility toward the federal government and its past role in domestic affairs and a preference for encouraging decision making and responsibility in the hands of the private sector and state and local governments. Although the Reagan forces did not seem especially interested in education per se, they pledged to eliminate the Department of Education. The general implication for education emerging from the Reagan campaign was that responsibility for higher education would devolve to a far greater extent upon the resources of private individuals and families and upon state and local authorities. The clearest statement of the direction the new administration might take was in a Heritage Foundation publication,

Mandate for Leadership: Policy Management in a Conservative Administration (Docksai and others 1979). The report proposed major changes in federal programs for elementary and secondary education as well as modification of the existing structure of federal policies and programs for higher education. It left no doubt about its posture toward the Department of Education:

> *In the short time the Department has been in existence, an established collection of literature has developed chronicling the administrative excesses of the Department, the wasted time, money, and energies that have failed to improve educational quality or extend its reach. For the most part, and given the most ideal of circumstances, the authors of this report would prefer to erase what Congress has done during the past two years* (Docksai and others 1979, p. 170).

Although very little could be done about the 1980 Amendments and legislation passed during the Carter administration could be modified only partially for 1981, spending levels in student aid programs in 1981 were 10 percent lower than in 1980 appropriations. Congress then passed stopgap legislation that cut education programs by another 5 percent from 1981.

The proposed higher education budget for fiscal year 1982 surprised the higher education associations and startled members of Congress who did not immediately perceive how the budget would affect higher education. The result was that, aside from the Guaranteed Student Loan Program, appropriations for higher education were reduced 12 percent in the 1982 budget (Stanfield 1982, p. 1262).

The Associations and the Reagan Budget for 1983
In late December 1981, after Congress had passed the stopgap spending resolution, the associations got a look at a preliminary copy of the 1983 budget. It called for a cut of 40 percent in Pell grants, from $2.3 billion to $1.4 billion, and proposed that three other higher education programs be discontinued.

With the experience of the 1982 cuts and the 1983 budget confronting them, the higher education associations organized and fought aggressively to prevent the cuts and the

The proposed higher education budget for fiscal year 1982 surprised the higher education associations and startled members of Congress. . . .

drastic consequences for higher education. Twenty higher education associations formed the Action Committee for Higher Education (ACHE) and undertook an immensely effective public relations campaign among their constituents to stave off the proposed reductions. ACHE was instrumental in persuading television networks, newspapers, and weekly news magazines that student aid was an issue of national importance. The committee conducted a successful grass-roots campaign to alert parents and students that student aid was in jeopardy. It put out a series of "how-to" pamphlets: "How to Lobby Your Congressman," "How to Write Letters to Your Local Newspaper," "How to Call a Press Conference," "How to Explain How This Proposal Impacts on Your Campus."

One Washington association official described the ensuing impact on Washington:

> *The Reagan administration tried to cut student aid in half. We organized a very careful grass-roots campaign, and the Hill has rarely seen such screaming. They heard from aunts, uncles, parents, students, faculty, college administrators, trustees. We'd walk around the Hill, and people would meet us, and they would say, "I've never seen anything like this. When are you going to turn it off?"*

As expected, the House Education and Labor Committee, with its consistent support for education programs, voted for increases for higher education programs. Unexpectedly, however, Republican conservatives like Jack Kemp and Orrin Hatch also came down on the side of student aid. Congress ignored the Reagan cuts and in some areas increased student aid. It overrode the president's veto. While the associations believed that their campaign to alert the grass roots had been successful, they were quick to acknowledge that it would not always work. In this successful instance of mobilizing the hinterlands, Congress was especially receptive to the wishes of the folks back home: (1) Elections were to take place in the fall; (2) almost no voters voiced their opposition; and (3) the clearest, loudest voices were those of middle-class citizens. Congress listened.

CURRENT ISSUES AND THE FUTURE: THE WASHINGTON COMMUNITY IN THE LAST HALF OF THE DECADE

The Present Environment

The Big Six plus One and the Washington higher education associations currently operate in a much more complex environment than they did in the 1960s and even in the 1970s. Thus, the structure of the community is also more complex.

Perhaps because of its size and visibility, higher education seems to be directly affected by more federal legislation, much of which is initiated for programs other than higher education and is not written with any thought concerning its possible effect on higher education. The higher education enterprise is not alone in this respect, but if the community is to deal with its complicated Washington environment, it must continually monitor government activities, disseminate relevant information to its members, find a community position if possible, and communicate that position to the appropriate targets in Congress and the administration. When it all works, the Washington association community is indeed a formidable spokesman for higher education.

A number of mechanisms have been established to monitor the federal government's activities; some have been discarded, others modified.

Federal relations offices

The upgrading of federal relations offices in all of the Big Six is one response to the increasingly complex world of Washington, and Saunders's organization of regular, frequent meetings of association federal relations officers is crucial to monitoring and the process of influence. The meetings are central in sounding out the community, fostering cooperation among the associations, and finding the basis for coordinated efforts. A major contribution is the establishment of policy research and analysis units, the most visible of which ACE initiated and now involves the associations working together in the Association Council for Policy Analysis and Research.

One indicator of the current sophistication and expertise in federal relations is the compilation and publication of ACE's "Higher Education Agendas," which have been published in the *Educational Record* over the years and sent as memos to the 96th, 97th, and 98th Congresses. The agendas present higher education's agreed-upon, overall priorities for a particular Congress and spell out specific community positions on particular issues that fall under the jurisdiction of the relevant committees in the House of Representatives and the Senate. The range of interests is wide—from issues like student aid that the higher education community would be expected to address to such seemingly far-removed issues as postal subsidies (ACE 1983, p. 5) and the bankruptcy laws (p. 12). Their targets include not only the House and Senate committees that deal directly with education and appropriations but also the Senate Commerce, Science, and Transportation Committee and the House Government Operations Committee.

ACE is not alone in this expertise and thorough research and in presenting higher education's positions. The other five of the Big Six are also noted for their depth, thoroughness, and capable presentations to Congress and the administration.

The division of labor

The immensity of the task—being on top of relevant legislation and the activities of the federal government—has led to important divisions of labor among the associations in the 1980s. One way of proceeding has been the roughly similar continuation of the "lead agency," the concept introduced by Roger Heyns in the 1970s. Now, however, the division of tasks is more informal, with a particular association assuming the responsibility for monitoring and informing the rest of the community in a particular area as its own interests dictate. At present, NAICU concentrates on tax problems, AAU on the health field, science, and \federal research grants and contracts, NASULGC on energy policies, and AASCU on urban affairs and the Servicemen's Opportunity College.

The division of labor has its cooperative aspects in the sharing of information with the other associations. The combination of the division of labor and cooperation means that associations might be designated to operate an activity jointly—as for the Academic Collective Bargaining Service coordinated by AAC, AASCU, and AACJC.

A further variation on this theme is the Association Council for Policy Analysis and Research (ACPAR). Comprised of 25 associations, its office and staff are operated by ACE, but its responsibilities are to the associations that are members. ACPAR's purposes have been to identify issues of importance to higher education, to bring them to national attention, to encourage coordination of research and analysis among the Washington associations, and to advise ACE's Policy and Analysis Division.* The Action Committee for Higher Education, the coalition of some 20 associations that was instrumental in persuading Congress to override President Reagan's veto in 1982, has had significant input from associations beyond the Big Six, including the Council for the Advancement and Support of Education. The Consortium for International Cooperation in Higher Education, comprised of members of associations with international programs, and the former Emergency Committee for Full Funding of Education have consolidated their efforts and become the Education Funding Committee, a large group representing a wide variety of educational interests. Thus, a pattern of dividing the labor and cooperating has emerged, involving groups usually smaller than the whole Washington education community but larger than only the Big Six.

Another division of labor is among the associations' federal relations officers. Individual officers are responsible for monitoring hearings in the House and the Senate, organizing presentations at hearings and other gatherings, speaking to individual Congressmen and Department of Education officials, and so on. Although the federal relations staff at any particular association is small, each can call on the support and services of the entire Washington higher education community.

This division of labor also calls forth a way of operating federal relations in the 1980s that is different from the pattern of the 1960s. If so much information is to be gathered, it must also be disseminated. The associations are much more open in their exchange of information than they were in the 1960s, and the community is much the richer for it.

In the mid-1980s, the American Council on Education is the center of efforts to coordinate the sectors of higher education through the association community. Its mandate to seek a unified course for higher education in Washington, its responsibilities for association relations, its role in organizing federal relations, and the prominent place ACE

*ACPAR 1982, 1984, public statements.

has in the various communitywide committees and policy-making groups all attest to the Council's position in the forefront. Even so, ACE is a partner in some recently formed associationwide committees that it did not initiate or that it joined only after the committees were formed.

The Brethren

One of the patterns of cooperation and division of labor among the associations is the current organization of the Big Six. It is a well-recognized, functional necessity that the full-time top executives of the major associations must see each other regularly—and to do so without the representatives of the satellite associations and without the elected leaders of their associations. Several mechanisms have been used toward this end in the past. Perhaps the original constituent members of the Council in 1918 were such a group. The Tuesday Luncheon Club of the 1960s had something of the quality for a period of time. The Secretariat of the 1960s and early 1970s was clearly a mechanism for the executive leaders of the major associations to gather, talk informally, and seek cooperation. Such groups have been subject to a loss of power and great erosion of their significance over time, however. A small group of the top leaders of the major associations is an attractive gathering, viewed as having valuable information, prestige, and perhaps even power, and other association leaders want to be included. Although a good reason is often apparent to include one or more other association leaders at some point, eventually the small, informal group becomes larger and more formal. The absentee rate of chief executive officers begins to rise precipitously. Staff members from the associations account for the majority of the attendees, and the group changes character. And the major association chief executives will be found to have formed a new, small, informal, exclusive forum for frank discussion, unencumbered by staff and representatives from the satellite associations. Meetings of the Brethren are the successor to the Secretariat of the 1980s. The Secretariat continues, but it is far larger than it was and it no longer serves as a forum for the Big Six and a few others to discuss significant events on the Washington higher education scene. If the Brethren begin to follow the pattern of the Secretariat, one may eventually find a new small group of the core associations, perhaps a "Brethren Born Again" or, given their penchant for rivalry as well as cooperation, "Siblings Six."

Associations and the wider world of interests

During the 1960s, some association watchers expressed concern that higher education was too insulated in Washington, that it would never count very much in Washington decision making until it was able to make common cause with larger, more powerful interest groups, particularly business and labor. In the 1980s, however, the associations have taken steps to broaden the reach of their interests, and ACE, for example, has organized a functioning and flourishing higher education–business forum and a similar set of activities with labor.

Community norms and the 1980s

The values and guidelines for action in the 1980s are an extension of the norms from the 1960s. The aim is still to find bases for cooperation while representing individual constituencies to the best of an association's ability. These norms have been elaborated and given new strength in the 1980s, however.

The publicly stated dictum from the 1960s that associations should consult with each other but not get in the way of each other's legislative objectives has been superseded by the much stronger doctrine that the community should not be surprised by other associations' activities and that they must seek concrete ways to coordinate their activities. They are backed by an association communications network that operates daily and is further strengthened by the often-voiced sentiment that each association understands: In governmental relations, the unstated meaning of a mutual veto among the associations is that either the associations cooperate or they face stalemate and destructive inactivity. Striking out on one's own begins to look like a lonely and risky enterprise.

Another corollary of the "no surprises" concept is that it should apply to relations with the federal government. Thus, when all else fails and divisions run deep, as one ranking association official put it: *It's our responsibility to go up on the Hill and say, "This is a matter of serious division in the community. This sector feels this way, and*

that sector feels that way for the following reasons."
That's a perfectly legitimate role.

The associations' realization in the 1960s that not only could the individual associations succeed without cooperating with other associations but also that the community needed the support and participation of its institutional leaders has developed into a working consensus that the grass roots must be cultivated and listened to and that the higher education community must take steps to cooperate with other major sectors of the society. It is now a realistic belief by association executives that successful coordination and cooperation have a tendency to be invisible and to occur daily. Some of their best and most successful work is not and will not be known by their constituents.

What Lies Ahead?

The publics and the independents
The most important current issue, and the one most likely to be most important in the near future, is the problem of student aid. The associations were able to cooperate and achieved considerable success in the reauthorization package of 1980. Though neither side considered it ideal, both private and public institutions thought they could live with it. The combined cooperative efforts of the public and private sectors were crucial in 1982 in preserving the student aid system, which looked as though it might disintegrate with the proposed legislation from the administration. In 1984, however, the inadequacies, problems, and conflicts embedded in the aid structure had developed to such an extent that the carefully negotiated and maintained cooperation resulting from the 1980 legislation was on the verge of serious disruption.

By 1984, the private institutions were widely concerned that they had made a bad deal in 1980, that the compromise package they had agreed to had not been funded in parts, and that they were worse off in 1984 as a result. Public institutions were not happy either, because they felt that the Pell grants should have been higher and that they should not have agreed to the half-cost limitations.

The haves and have nots
Although one response to the alleged differences between

haves and have nots is that most institutions are now and/
or will be have nots in the future, it is still an issue, particularly in relation to the independent institutions. Because
the distinction involves contrasts not only in size and
resources but also in interests, the possibility of new, sepa-
ratist national associations, threatening the unity of the
independent sector, continues.

Other issues, large and small

The list of concerns facing associations is long and the
issues complicated. The immense federal debt and its
potential negative consequences seem to place in jeopardy
all domestic programs, including higher education. The
changing tax structure, with its implications for reducing
incentives to contribute to nonprofit organizations, looms
on the horizon. The necessity for increased funding and the
competitiveness of institutions for research funds threaten
the peer system of review at the federal level. Academic
control of intercollegiate athletics provides yet another
potentially divisive arena for the higher education sectors,
and even the National Center for Higher Education, the
building at One Dupont Circle whose purpose is the
improvement of communication and coordination among
the associations by having them under one roof, on occasion is the basis for an "issue" ("Who owns the building?"
"What is its purpose?").

Despite past successes and current capabilities, this
group has by no means resolved its problems, nor does it
really have much control over what will happen to the
higher education enterprise in Washington in the future. In
the final analysis, the higher education community is essentially a bit player, able to come on stage at crucial
moments and make a difference but not in charge of the
plot, the tempo of the action, or even the scenery. At the
macro level, threats of war, depression, international
crises, inflation, the national debt, ideological swings right
and left, changes in the national mood, and specific political events all occur continually—and unpredictably—and
higher education can do nothing about them except to
attempt to cope. On a micro level, legislation regularly
passes that has very significant consequences for higher
education, but often decision makers do not take those
consequences into consideration.

In the mid-1980s, the associations can look back with considerable satisfaction at having been importantly involved in federal higher education policy. Despite education's having been on short rations since 1972 and having experienced a number of disappointments, solid successes occurred in 1976, 1978, 1980, and 1982. The associations can point with some pride to two major accomplishments. They were influential in helping to shape and preserve federal funding for higher education (particularly student aid), and in the process they transformed themselves from a passive, partially informed, often divided, nonpolitical community into a keenly attentive, highly informed, and skillfully assertive body of associations participating daily in Washington higher education policy and events. Although they realistically understand that they will probably never rival the resources and clout enjoyed by some of the larger associations representing business, labor, and agriculture, they have reason to believe that a good deal of working machinery is in place and operational and that the associations have the personnel and organizational skill and knowledge to move quickly and effectively when the occasion arises.

REFERENCES

The ERIC Clearinghouse on Higher Education abstracts and indexes the current literature on higher education for the National Institute of Education's monthly bibliographic journal, *Resources in Education*. Most of these publications are available through the ERIC Document Reproduction Service (EDRS). For publications cited in this bibliography that are available from EDRS, ordering number and price are included. Readers who wish to order a publication should write to the ERIC Document Reproduction Service, 3900 Wheeler Avenue, Alexandria, Virginia 22304. When ordering, please specify the document number. Documents are available as noted in microfiche (MF) and paper copy (PC). Because prices are subject to change, it is advisable to check the latest issue of *Resources in Education* for current cost based on the number of pages in the publication.

Advisory Commission on Intergovernmental Relations. 1981. "The Evolution of a Problematic Partnership: The Feds and Higher Ed." In *The Federal Role in the Federal System: The Dynamics of Growth*. Washington, D.C.: ACIR, U.S. Department of Education, National Institute of Education, Educational Resource and Information Center. ED 209 977. 67 pp. MF–$1.19; PC–$7.39.

Aldrich, Howard E., and Pfeffer, Jeffrey. 1976. "Environments of Organizations." *Annual Review of Sociology* 2: 79–105.

Almond, Gabriel. 1983. "Corporatism, Pluralism, and Professional Memory." *World Politics* 35(2): 245–60.

American Council on Education. 1966. *Annual Report*. Washington, D.C.: ACE.

———. 1969. *Annual Report*. Washington, D.C.: ACE.

———. 1976. *Annual Report*. Washington, D.C.: ACE.

———. 1979a. "Activities Report." Washington, D.C.: ACE, Division of Governmental Relations.

———. Winter 1979b. "A Higher Education Agenda for the 96thCongress." *Educational Record* 60(1): 103–21.

———. Spring 1981. "A Higher Education Agenda for the 97th Congress." *Educational Record* 62(2): 8–17.

———. 1983. "A Higher Education Agenda for the 98th Congress." Memo to members of the 98th Congress.

Association Council for Policy Analysis and Research. 1982. *The National Investment in Higher Education*. Washington, D.C.: ACPAR.

———. 1984. *America Has a New Urgency*. Washington, D.C.: ACPAR.

Babbidge, Homer D., Jr., and Rosenzweig, Robert. 1962. *The Federal Interest in Higher Education*. New York: McGraw-Hill.

Babchuck, Nicholas, and Warriner, Charles K. 1965. "Introduction." *Sociological Inquiry* 35(2): 135–37.

Bailey, Stephen K. 1975. *Education Interest Groups in the Nation's Capital*. Washington, D.C.: American Council on Education.

———. 1978. "The Peculiar Mixture: Public Norms and Private Spaces." In *Government Regulation of Higher Education,* edited by Walter Hobbs. Cambridge, Mass.: Ballinger.

Baker, Donald P., and Barnes, Bart. 28 January 1980. "College Lobbyists Flocking Here in Quest for Funds." *Washington Post*.

Bloland, Harland G. 1968. "National Associations and the Shaping of Federal Higher Education Policy." *Sociology of Education* 41(2): 156–77.

———. 1969a. *Higher Education Associations in a Decentralized System*. Berkeley, Cal.: Center for Research and Development in Higher Education. ED 029 619. 214 pp. MF–$1.19; PC–$18.72.

———. 1969b. "The Politicization of Higher Education Organizations: Assets and Liabilities." In *Agony and Promise: Current Issues in Higher Education,* edited by G. Kerry Smith. San Francisco: Jossey-Bass.

Bloland, Harland G., and Bloland, Sue M. 1974. *American Learned Societies in Transition*. New York: McGraw-Hill.

Bloland, Harland G., and Wilson, O. Meredith. 1971. *Report on the Higher Education Secretariat Community*. Washington, D.C.: Secretariat.

Breneman, David W., and Finn, Chester E., Jr., eds. 1978. *Public Policy and Private Higher Education*. Washington, D.C.: Brookings Institution.

Brittan, J., and Freeman, J. 1980. "Organizational Proliferation and Density of Dependent Selection." In *The Organizational Life Cycle,* edited by John Kimberly, Robert Miles, and Associates. San Francisco: Jossey-Bass.

Carlson, Edgar M. 1976. "The National Representation Project: A Report and an Accounting." *Liberal Learning* 62(2): 274–83.

Cheit, Earl F. 1971. *The New Depression in Higher Education*. New York: McGraw-Hill.

Child, John, and Kieser, Alfred. 1981. "The Development of Organizations over Time." In *Handbook of Organizational Design,* vol. 1, edited by Paul Nystrom and William Starbuck. New York: Oxford University Press.

Clark, Peter B., and Wilson, James Q. 1961. "Incentive Systems: A Theory of Organization." *Administrative Science Quarterly* 6(2): 129–66.

Commager, Henry Steele, ed. 1947. *Alexis de Tocqueville's Democracy in America*. New York: Oxford University Press.

Cosand, Joseph P.; Gurin, Gerald; Peterson, Marvin W.; and Brister, Frank R. 1980. *Presidential Views of Higher Education's National Institutional Membership Associations: Summary Report*. Ann Arbor: University of Michigan, Center for the Study of Higher Education.

Coser, Lewis, 1956. *The Functions of Social Conflict*. New York: Free Press of Glencoe.

Council for the Advancement and Support of Education. 1982–83. *Annual Report*. Washington, D.C.: CASE.

Dobbins, Charles G., ed. 1968. *American Council on Education: Leadership and Chronology, 1918–1968*. Washington, D.C.: American Council on Education.

Docksai, Ronald F., and Others. 1979. "The Department of Education." In *Mandate for Leadership: Policy Management in a Conservative Administration*. Washington, D.C.: Heritage Foundation.

Emerson, Richard M. 1962. "Power-Dependence Relations." *American Sociological Review* 27(1): 31–34.

Finn, Chester E., Jr. 1978. *Scholars, Dollars, and Bureaucrats*. Washington, D.C.: Brookings Institution.

———. September 1980. "The Future of Liberal Education's Liberal Consensus." *Change* 12(6): 25–30.

Fretwell, E. K. October 1980. "A Report to the Coordinating Committee from the Subcommittee on Association Relations." Washington, D.C.: American Council on Education.

———. Winter 1981. "Association Report." *Educational Record* 62(1): 78–80.

Gladieux, Lawrence E. 1977. "Education Lobbies Come into Their Own." *Change* 9(3): 42–43.

Gladieux, Lawrence E., and Wolanin, Thomas R. 1976. *Congress and the Colleges*. Lexington, Mass.: D. C. Heath.

———. 1978. "Federal Politics." In *Public Policy and Private Higher Education,* edited by David Breneman and Chester E. Finn, Jr. Washington, D.C.: Brookings Institution.

Hamilton, Bette Everett. 1977. "Federal Policy Networks for Postsecondary Education." Ph.D. dissertation, University of Michigan.

Hayes, Michael T. 1978. "The Semi-Sovereign Pressure Groups: A Critique of Current Theory and an Alternative Typology." *Journal of Politics* 40(1): 134–61.

Heyns, Roger. 1973. "The National Educational Establishment." *Educational Record* 54(2): 93–99.

———. 1977. "The President's Report." In *ACE Annual Report 1976*. Washington, D.C.: American Council on Education.

Hobbs, Walter C., ed. 1978. *Government Regulation in Higher Education*. Cambridge, Mass.: Ballinger.

Honey, John C. December 1972. "The Election, Politics, and Higher Education." *Science* 78(4067): 1243.

———. 1979. "Higher Education's Great Opportunity." *Educational Record* 60(3): 329–35.

Honey, John C., and Crowley, John C. 1972. "The Future of the American Council on Education: A Report on Its Governmental and Related Activities." Washington, D.C.: ACE.

Hook, Janet. 25 August 1980. "A Compromise Student-Loan Plan Voted by House-Senate Conferees." *Chronicle of Higher Education* 22(1): 17–18.

Hrebener, Ronald, and Scott, Ruth K. 1982. *Interest Group Politics in America*. Englewood Cliffs, N.J.: Prentice-Hall.

Hunt, Susan. February 1977. "NAICU's Growing Pains." *Change* 9(2): 50–51.

Kimberly, John R. 1980. "Initiation, Innovation, and Institutionalization of the Creation Process." In *The Organizational Life Cycle,* edited by John Kimberly, Robert Miles, and Associates. San Francisco: Jossey-Bass.

Kimberly, John R.; Miles, Robert H.; and Associates, eds. 1980. *The Organizational Life Cycle*. San Francisco: Jossey-Bass.

King, Lauriston. 1972. "The Vanishing Grantsman." *Change* 4(4): 8–9.

———. 1975. *The Washington Lobbyists for Higher Education*. Lexington, Mass.: Lexington Books.

Lipset, Seymour M. 1960. *Political Man*. New York: Doubleday.

Lipset, Seymour; Trow, Martin; and Coleman, James. 1962. *Union Democracy*. Garden City, N.Y.: Anchor Books.

McClelland, David S. 1965. "Need Achievement and Entrepreneurship: A Longitudinal Study." *Journal of Personality and Social Psychology* 1(4): 389–92.

McConnell, Grant. 1966. *Private Power and American Democracy*. New York: Knopf.

McNamara, William. 1976a. "Backing Demands with Data." *Change* 8(9): 46–47.

———. 1976b. "The Wallflower Dances: The Education Lobby Steps Out." *CASE Currents* 2(1): 4–7.

————. March 1978. "The Tax Credit Debate." *Change* 10(3): 44–45 + .

Magarrell, Jack. 5 February 1979. "Academe and Industry Weigh a New Alliance." *Chronicle of Higher Education* 17(21): 1 + .

Michels, Robert. 1915. *Political Parties.* New York: Dover.

Moe, Terry M. 1980. *The Organization of Interests.* Chicago: University of Chicago Press.

————. 1981. "Toward a Broader View of Interest Groups." *Journal of Politics* 43: 531–43.

Morse, John F. 1969. "The Federal Role in Education: One View." *Proceedings: Symposium on Financing Higher Education.* Atlanta: Southern Regional Education Board.

Moynihan, Daniel P. 1975. "The Politics of Higher Education." *Daedalus* 104(1): 128–47.

Murray, Michael A. 1976. "Defining the Higher Education Lobby." *Journal of Higher Education* 57(1): 79–92.

Nall, Frank. 1967. "National Associations." In *The Emergent American Society,* edited by W. Warner, D. B. Unwalla, and J. H. Trimm. New Haven: Yale University Press.

Newman, Frank, et al. 1971. *Report on Higher Education.* Washington, D.C.: Department of Health, Education, and Welfare. ED 049 718. 136 pp. MF–$1.19; PC not available EDRS.

Nystrom, Paul, and Starbuck, William, eds. 1981. *Handbook of Organizational Design,* vol. 1. New York: Oxford University Press.

Olson, Mancur. 1971. *The Logic of Collective Action.* Rev. ed. New York: Schocken.

Peltason, Jack W. 1978. "Five Year Planning: Initial Steps." *Memorandum* to ACE Board of Directors.

Peterson, Richard A. 1981. "Entrepreneurship and Organization." In *Handbook of Organizational Design,* vol. 1, edited by Paul Nystrom and William Starbuck. New York: Oxford University Press.

Pettit, Lawrence K. 1965. "The Policy Process in Congress: Passing the Higher Education Academic Facilities Act of 1963." Ph.D. dissertation, University of Wisconsin.

Rivlin, Alice. 1969. *Toward a Long-Range Plan for Federal Financial Support of Higher Education: A Report to the President.* Washington, D.C.: Department of Health, Education, and Welfare.

Rose, Arnold. 1955. "Voluntary Associations under Conditions of Competition and Conflict." *Social Forces* 34(2): 159–63.

Rosenzweig, Robert. 1965. "Education Lobbies and Federal Legislation." In *Challenge and Change in American Education,* edited by Seymour Harris. Berkeley, Cal.: McCutchan.

Salisbury, Robert H. 1969. "An Exchange Theory of Interest Groups." *Midwest Journal of Political Science* 13(1): 1–32.

———. 1984. "Interest Representation: The Dominance of Institutions." *American Political Science Review* 78(1): 64–76.

Saunders, Charles B., Jr. 1976. "The Student Aid Merry-Go-Round." *Change* 8(7): 44–45.

———. 21 March 1978. Testimony before the Committee on Governmental Affairs. U.S. Congress, House of Representatives.

———. 1981. "The Role of the National Associations." *New Directions for Institutional Advancement* (12): 49–58.

———. 1983. "Reshaping Federal Aid to Higher Education." In *The Crisis in Higher Education,* edited by Joseph Froomkin. New York: The Academy of Political Science.

Schattschneider, Elmer E. 1960. *The Semi-Sovereign People.* New York: Holt, Rinehart, and Winston.

Schumpeter, Joseph. 1934. *Theory of Economic Development.* Cambridge, Mass.: Harvard University Press.

———. 1947. "The Creative Response in Economic History."

Schuster, Jack H. 1982. "Out of the Frying Pan: The Politics of Education in a New Era." *Phi Delta Kappan* 63(9): 583–91.

Scully, Malcolm G. December 1979. "Michigan Center, 'Gang of Six' to Study Performance of Eight Educational Associations." *Chronicle of Higher Education* 19(15): 9–10.

Semas, Philip W. 30 October 1972. "Few Changes Thus Far in Higher Education's Washington 'Umbrella.' " *Chronicle of Higher Education* 7(6): 3.

Sills, David L. 1968. "Voluntary Associations: Sociological Aspects." In *International Encyclopedia of the Social Sciences,* vol. 16, edited by David L. Sills. New York: Macmillan/Free Press.

Smelser, Neil J. 1963. "Mechanisms for Change and Adjustments to Change." In *Industrialization and Society,* edited by Wilbert E. Moore and Bert F. Hoselitz. Paris: UNESCO.

Somit, Albert, and Tanenhaus, Joseph. 1964. *American Political Science: A Profile of a Discipline.* New York: Atherton Press.

Stanfield, Rochelle L. 1 April 1978. "The Taxpayers' Revolt: Part II—Education Aid for Everybody?" *National Journal* 10(13): 509–14.

———. 17 July 1982. "Student Aid Lobby Learns New Tricks to Fight Reagan's Spending Cutbacks." *National Journal* 14(29): 1261–64.

Stewart, Donald M. Forthcoming. *Politics of Higher Education: A Study of the American Council on Education*. San Francisco: Jossey-Bass.

Stinchcombe, Arthur. 1965. "Social Structure and Organizations." In *Handbook of Organizations,* edited by James G. March. Chicago: Rand McNally.

Sundquist, James L. 1968. *Politics and Policy: The Eisenhower, Kennedy, and Johnson Years*. Washington, D.C.: Brookings Institution.

Truman, David B. 1955. *The Governmental Process*. New York: Knopf.

Tuttle, William M., Jr. 1970. "Higher Education and the Federal Government: The Triumph, 1942–1945." *The Record* 71(3): 485–99.

U.S. Congress, House of Representatives. 17 October 1979. Education Amendments of 1980, H.R. 520. 96th Congress, 1st Session.

Walker, Jack L. 1983. "The Origins and Maintenance of Interest Groups in America." *The American Political Science Review* 77(2): 390–405.

Warren, Roland L. 1967. "The Interorganizational Field as a Focus for Investigation." *Administrative Science Quarterly* 2(3): 396–419.

Watkins, Beverly. 10 July 1978. "American Council to Reorganize." *Chronicle of Higher Education* 16(18): 5.

Wilson, G. 1981. *Interest Groups in the United States*. New York: Oxford University Press.

Wilson, James Q. 1973. *Political Organization*. New York: Basic Books.

Wilson, John T. 1982. *Higher Education and the Washington Scene: 1982*. Chicago: University of Chicago Press.

Wolanin, Thomas. October 1976. "The National Higher Education Associations: Political Resources and Style." *Phi Delta Kappan* 58(2): 181–84.

INDEX

A

AAC (see Association of American Colleges)

AACJC (see American Association of Community and Junior Colleges)

AAMC (see Association of American Medical Colleges)

AASCU (see American Association of State Colleges and Universities)

AAU (see Association of American Universities)

AAUP (see American Association of University Professors)

Academic Collective Bargaining Service, 84

Accreditation, 3

Accreditation associations, 13

ACE (see American Council on Education)

ACHE (see Action Committee for Higher Education)

ACPAR (see Association Council for Policy Analysis and Research)

Action Committee for Higher Education (ACHE), 82, 85

Adult education: AACJC support, 22

AERA (see American Educational Research Association)

AFL-CIO, 44

AFT (see American Federation of Teachers)

Age Discrimination in Employment Act of 1967, 53

Agricultural education: NASULGC position, 18

Aid to Developing Institutions, 38

American Association of Community and Junior Colleges (AACJC)

    Academic Collective Bargaining Service, 84

    "Big Six," xix

    community activity support, 62

    conflict with AASCU/NASULGC, 41

    description, 21–22

    dues, 76

    reprimand, 42

American Association of State Colleges and Universities (AASCU)

    Academic Collective Bargaining Service, 84

    alliance with AACJC, 21

    "Big Six," xix, 15

    community activity support, 62

    conflict with AACJC, 41

    description, 19–20, 75

    lead agency responsibility, 84

    position on BEOGs, 73

representation of "have nots," 55, 56
tax credit split with AAC, 19
American Association of University Professors (AAUP), 13, 40
American Bar Association, 23
American Council on Education (ACE)
    AACJC reprimand, 42
    Academic Affairs, 60
    ACPAR operation, 84–85
    Administrative Affairs, 60
    "Big Six," xix, 15
    Business-Higher Education Forum, 87
    Commission on Federal Relations, 40–41
    commitment to state government relations, 69
    Coordinating Committee, 61
    coordinator role, 49, 51, 60, 76–78, 85–86
    description, 16–17
    distribution of material benefits, 10
    dues, 76
    Division of External Relations, 69
    Division of Governmental Relations, 58–59, 69
    Division of Institutional Relations, 69
    Division of International Relations, 69
    Division of Policy Analysis, 69, 85
    government relations, 29–30, 51, 57–59
    Heyns presidency, 57–62
    Higher Education and National Affairs, xx
    institutional interest fairness, 4
    Leadership Development, 60
    organizing, 29
    Peltason presidency, 68–69
    Policy Analysis Service, 59
    representation of community-wide interests, 55, 75
    representation of "haves" and "have nots," 56
    reorganization, 69
    role on construction loans, 33
    role on President's Committee, 30
    role on Reauthorization Act, 73
    Secretariat, 26, 40, 42, 61–62, 86
    size, 21
    stated goals, 10–11
    statement on institutional aid, 38
    study on goals, 77–78
    support by AAC, 45

support for COFHE report, 66
support for Department of Education, 72
support for Emergency Committee, 44
Women in Higher Education, 60
work with AASCU, 20
American Educational Research Association (AERA), 13
American Federation of Teachers (AFT), 70, 71
American Medical Association, 23
American Political Science Association, 24
American Sociological Association, 13
Associated Colleges of the Midwest, 23–24
Association Council for Policy Analysis and Research (ACPAR),
    83–85
Association of American Agricultural Colleges and Experiment
    Stations, 18
Association of American Colleges (AAC)
    Academic Collective Bargaining Service, 84
    affiliation with ACE, 45
    "Big Six," xix, 15
    description, 19
    politicization/NAICU, 63–65
    position on federal aid, 34, 38, 44–45
    representation of "have nots," 56
    representation of specialized interests, 55
    representation on ACE board, 17
    satellite associations, 23
Association of American Law Schools, 23
Association of American Medical Colleges (AAMC), 23
Association of American Universities (AAU)
    "Big Six," xix, 15
    change in membership incentives, 11
    Council on Federal Relations established, 63
    description, 22
    dues, 76
    government relations, 65
    institutionally tied, 13
    lead agency responsibility, 84
    representation of "haves," 55, 56
    satellite associations, 23
    support for COFHE report, 66
Associations
    "Big Six," or core, xix, xx, 14–15, 24, 86
    classification, 13–14, 24

---

cooperation with federal decision making, 28
decision making, 4
development, xix–xx
division of tasks, 84–86
dues, 76
federal relations offices, 83–84
formation, 5–7
image, 67–69, 74
location in Washington, D.C., 5
material benefits, 10
membership, 1–4, 7–12
norms/consensus, 39–42, 87
outlook, 89–90
outreach of interests, 87
"peripheral lobbies," 24
purposive benefits, 10–11
relationship to social/political order, 2
satellite lobbies, 22–24
teaching activities, 1
transition period, 42–47
Atwell (Robert), 69

B
Bailey (Stephen K.), 58
Basic Educational Opportunity Grants (BEOGs), 51, 72–74
Benefits: distribution of, 10
BEOGs (see Basic Educational Opportunity Grants)
"Big Six" associations, xix, xx, 10, 14–15, 25, 34, 40, 58, 79, 83–86
Black colleges
    NASULGC position, 18
    satellite association membership, 23
Boyer (Ernest), 80
Brademas (John), 50, 67
"Brethren, The," 62, 86–87
Brewster (Kingman), 74
Brookings Institution, 24, 39, 80
Building programs, 24

C
Carlson (Edgar), 65
Carter Administration, 70, 71, 79, 81
CASE (see Council for the Advancement and Support of
    Education)

Categorical aid programs, 24, 38

Catholic colleges (see Church related colleges)

CGS (see Council of Graduate Schools)

Change Magazine, xx

Chief executives: need to meet, 86

Chronicle of Higher Education, xx

Church related colleges

AAC representation, 19

opposition to federal aid, 34, 45, 63

representation of "have nots," 56

satellite association members, 23

CICHE (see Consortium for International Cooperation in Higher Education)

Civil Rights Act of 1964, 53

Clark (Joseph S.), 32–33, 42

Classification schemes, 13–16, 24

Coalition building/action, 35, 85

Coalition of Independent University Students (COIUS), 67

COFHE (see Consortium on Financing Higher Education)

COIUS (see Coalition of Independent University Students)

College Housing Loan Program, 72

College presidents

benefits of AAU membership, 11

concern over regulation, 52–53, 74

dissent on AAC position, 45

expertise in NASULGC, 18

Gang of Six (Gang of Ten), 76, 77

role in ACE policy-making, 40

role in federal policy-making, 31–32, 64–65

view of associations, 77–78

College Service Bureau, 23

College Work Study programs, 72

Community colleges: AACJC representation, 21

Community service: AACJC support, 22

Complexity theory (association formation), 5–6

Congress (see also Federal relations; "House" and "Senate" headings), 25, 32, 50

Consensus, 40–41, 59

Consortia, 23

Consortium for International Cooperation in Higher Education (CICHE), 85

Consortium on Financing of Higher Education (COFHE), 66

Constitutional law, 27

Construction loans, 24, 32–33, 37

Cooperative mechanisms: government/associations, 39–41

"Core lobbies" (see "Big Six")

Cosand (Joseph), 76

Council for the Advancement and Support of Education (CASE), 85

Council for the Advancement of Private Independent Four-Year Institutions, 23

Council of Graduate Schools (CGS), 13, 23

Council of Protestant Colleges and Universities, 23, 40

D

De Toqueville: view of associations, 2

Democratic expression, 2–4

Department of Education, 26, 71–72, 79, 80, 81

Department of Health, Education, and Welfare, 25, 30, 43

Department of Housing and Urban Development, 72

Department of Labor, 43

Developing institutions: federal aid, 38

Disturbance theory (association formation), 5–6

Division of labor, 85–86

Doctoral degrees: awarded in NASULGC institutions, 18

Drucker (Peter), 80

Dues, 76

E

ECS (see Education Commission of the States)

Education Amendments of 1972, 25, 26, 37, 50, 51, 52, 67

Education Amendments of 1976, 67, 79

Education Amendments of 1980, 72–74, 79, 81

Education Commission of the States (ECS), 58

Education Funding Committee, 85

Educational opportunity grants, 38

Educational Record, 83

Elementary secondary education associations, 28, 35

Elementary secondary education interests, 71

Emergency Committee for Full Funding of Education, 36, 43–44, 46, 85

Environmental Protection Agency, 53

Equal educational opportunity, 28, 37

Equal Employment Opportunity Act of 1964, 38, 53

Equal Pay Act of 1963, 53

Entrepreneurial theory (association formation), 5, 7

Executive Order 11246, 53

F

Faculty organizations, 13

Family Educational Rights and Privacy Act of 1974, 53

Federal aid (see also Student Financial Aid), 20, 31–34, 37–39, 43–47

Federal government
  grants, 18
  relationship to, xix
  role in higher education, 26, 28–32, 80–82

Federal legislation (see also specific acts), 25–26

"Federal Programs for Higher Education: Needed Next Steps" (ACE), 38

Federal regulation, 23, 26, 51–53, 74

Federal relations (see also Lobbying)
  ACE Commission, 40–41
  AAU role, 65
  buildup, 51, 83–86
  development in 1970s, 56–62
  division of labor, 85
  improved image, 73

Federation of State Associations of Independent Colleges and Universities (FSAICU), 64–65

Financial aid (see Student financial aid)

First Amendment, 27

Ford (William), 70, 73

Ford Administration, 54

Ford Foundation, 79

Fourth Amendment, 27

"Free rider" problem, 8

FSAICU (see Federation of State Associations of Independent Colleges and Universities)

Fulbright program (ACE), 69

G

G.I. Bill of 1944, 30, 52

"Gang of Six" ("Gang of Ten"), 76–78

Glazer (Nathan), 80

Government relations (see Federal relations)

Governmental Relations Luncheon Group, 39–40

Graduate study
  AACJC position, 21, 62
  AAU position, 22, 62
  ACE position, 62

NASULGC position, 18, 62
    special interest associations, 23
Grant proposal advisors, 24
Green (Edith), 50
Guaranteed Student Loan Program, 81

H

Handicapped: aid to, 53
Hatch (Orrin), 82
Haves and have nots, 54–56, 88–89
HENA (see *Higher Education and National Affairs*)
Heritage Foundation, 80
Heyns (Roger), 51, 57–62, 68, 84
Hicks (Weimer), 64
Higher education
    centralization/decentralization, 28–29
    Congressional action, 25
    federal role, 26, 28–32
    financial problems, 47, 49
    fragmentation, 13–14
    growth in 1960s, 37
    growth patterns/interests, 6
    haves and have nots, 54–56, 88–89
    "liberal consensus," 26, 79–80
    mission, 34
    national defense role, 27
    state primacy, 27
Higher Education Act of 1965, 25, 26, 37, 38, 42, 50
"Higher Education Agendas," 83
Higher Education Amendments of 1976, 67
Higher Education and National Affairs (HENA), xx
Higher Education Reauthorization Act of 1980, 72–75, 88
Higher Educational Facilities Act of 1963, 25, 37, 63
Hill (Lister), 30
Honey (John C.), 51
Honey-Crowley Report, 51, 59, 67
Hook (Sidney), 80
House Education and Labor Committee, 25, 73, 82
House Government Operations Committee, 84
House of Representatives, 25, 26, 33, 43, 50
House Rules Committee, 63
House Special Subcommittee on Education, 25, 50
House Subcommittee on Postsecondary Education, 25, 73

"How-to" pamphlets: student aid lobbying, 82
Howe (Harold), 80

I

Independent sector (see National Association of Independent
   Colleges and Universities; Private sector)
Institutional aid, 39, 50
Institutional autonomy: role of associations, 3
Institutional types, 6
Institutionally tied associations, 13, 15
International education
       AASCU position, 20
       NASULGC position, 18
"Iron Law of Oligarchy," 3–4

J

Johnson Administration, 35, 38, 43
Junior colleges: AACJC representation, 21

K

Kemp (Jack), 82
Kennedy Administration, 37, 43
Kerr (Clark), 80
Kidd (Charles), 63

L

Land-grant institutions, 18
"Lead agency" concept, 84–85
Leadership, 9, 11–12
Learned societies, 1, 4, 13, 24
Legislation
       Age Discrimination in Employment Act of 1967, 53
       Civil Rights Act of 1964, 53
       Equal Employment Opportunity Act of 1964, 38, 53
       Equal Pay Act of 1963, 53
       Family Educational Rights and Privacy Act of 1974, 53
       Higher Education Act of 1965, 25, 26, 37, 38, 42, 50
       Higher Education Reauthorization Act of 1980, 72–75, 88
       Higher Educational Facilities Act of 1964, 25, 37, 63
       Middle Income Student Assistance Act of 1978, 70–71, 79
       Morrill Act of 1862, 29
       National Defense Act of 1916, 29

National Defense Education Act of 1958 (NDEA), 25, 30, 37

Occupational Safety and Health Act of 1970, 53

Liberal arts

AAC representation, 19, 65

need for special representation, 45

"Liberal consensus" of higher education, 26, 79–80

Librarians, 25

Libraries: federal aid, 38

Lobbying (see also Federal relations)

activist perspective, 35–36

coalitions, 44

origins, 27

pragmatic realism, 35

proposal by Clark, 32–33

reluctance toward, xix

success in student aid, 82

traditional approach, 34–35

M

Madison (James): views of factionalism, 3

Major associations (see "Big Six")

Mandate for Leadership: Policy Management in a Conservative Administration, 81

Membership in associations

collective action motives, 7–8

cost, 76

material incentives, 10

necessity, 75

questions of benefits, 7

perception of efficacy, 9

pluralistic motives, 7–9

purposive incentives, 10–11

solidary incentives, 11–12

tangible private benefits, 9

theoretical motives, 1–4, 7–10

Middle Income Student Assistance Act of 1978, 70–71, 79

Military training, 29, 84

Monitoring hearings, 85

Morrill Act of 1862, 29

Morse (John), 40, 58

Morse (Wayne), 43

Morse Group, 40–41

Moynihan (Daniel), 67, 70

N

NACUBO (see National Association of College and University Business Officers)

NAICU (see National Association of Independent Colleges and Universities)

NASULGC (see National Association of State Universities and Land-Grant Colleges)

National Association of Admissions Officers, 24

National Association of College and University Business Officers (NACUBO), 58

National Association of Independent Colleges and Universities (NAICU)
    "Big Six," xix, 15, 58
    establishment, 65–66
    formation as lobbying group, 46, 75
    lead agency responsibility: taxes, 84
    representation of "haves" and "have nots," 56
    satellite associations, 23
    Secretariat, 66

National Association of State Universities, 18

National Association of State Universities and Land-Grant Colleges (NASULGC)
    alliance with AACJC, 21
    "Big Six," xix, 15
    community activity support, 62
    conflict with AACJC, 41
    description, 17–18
    lead agency responsibility: energy, 84
    longevity, 26
    origins, 29
    position on undergraduate scholarships, 41
    representation of "haves," 56
    representation on ACE board, 17
    satellite associations, 23
    similarity to AASCU, 20
    tax credit split with AAC, 19

National Catholic Educational Association, 23

National Center for Higher Education, 15, 26, 78, 89

National Commission on Accreditation, 40

National Council for Independent Colleges and Universities (NCICU), 65

National defense, 27, 30, 37

National Defense Act of 1916, 29
National Defense Education Act of 1958 (NDEA), 25, 30, 37
National Education Association (NEA), 44, 59, 70, 71, 72
National Foundation on the Arts and Humanities, 72
National Student Association (NSA), 13, 67
National Student Education Fund, 67
National Student Lobby, 67
NCICU (see National Council for Independent Colleges and Universities)
NDEA (see National Defense Education Act of 1958)
NEA (see National Education Association)
New York Times, 79
Nixon Administration, 35, 43, 49, 54
Norms, 41–42, 87–88
NSA (see National Student Association)

O

Occupational groups, 24
Occupational Safety and Health Act of 1970, 53
Office of Education, 24, 25, 40, 41, 43
Ohio State University, 23
Oligarchy: presence in associations, 3–4
Organizational life cycles, 5
Ostar (Allan), 20

P

Packwood (Robert), 70
Part-time students, 21
Peer review: grant proposals, 3
Pell (Claiborne), 25, 50, 67, 74
Pell grants, 20, 70, 81, 88
Peltason (Jack), 68–69, 71, 77
"Peripheral lobbies," 24
Policy analysis, 59, 69
Policy formation, 24–28
Political benefits of membership, 10
Political factors (see also Lobbying)
    distribution of information, 10
    perspectives of higher education, 33–36
    types of programs/issues, 24–25
Powell (Adam Clayton), 25
Presidential Views of Higher Education's National Institutional Membership Associations, 77

Presidents (see College presidents)

"President's club" (AAU), 22

President's Committee on Education Beyond the High School, 30–31, 42

Private sector (see also National Association of Independent Colleges and Universities)

      federal aid, 37, 53–55

      politicization, 63–67

      position on construction loans, 32

      revenues, 27

Professional associations, 23

Professional education, 23

Protestant colleges (see Church related colleges)

Public sector (see also American Association of Community and Junior Colleges; American Association of State Colleges and Universities; National Association of State Universities and Land-Grant Colleges)

      community changes and attitudes, 62

      position on BEOGs, 72–73

      position on construction loans, 32

Public/private conflict: student aid, 53, 72–73, 88

Public/private nondiscrimination, 28, 29

Q

Quie (Albert), 50

R

Reagan Administration, 26, 28, 79–82, 85

Regional consortia, 23

Research

      AACJC position, 21

      AAU position, 22

      NASULGC position, 18

      special interest associations, 23

Research associations, 13

Research universities: AAU role, 11

Reserve Officers Training Corps, 29

Reward systems, 4

Richardson (Elliott), 30

S

Saunders (Charles B.), 58, 83

Secretariat (see American Council on Education/Secretariat)

Segregation, 37

Senate, 25

Senate Commerce, Science, and Transportation Committee, 84

Servicemen's Opportunity College, 84

Small colleges (see also Association of American Colleges; National Association of Independent Colleges and Universities), 66

Special Committee on Education, 25

Special interest associations, 22

Special task associations, 13

Special task groups, 24

Sputnik, 30

State colleges and universities (see American Association of State Colleges and Universities; Public sector)

State primacy, 27

State Student Incentive Grants, 73

State systems, 23

State Universities Association, 18

State University of New York, 23

Stated goals, 10–11

Student associations, 67

Student financial aid

    AACJC position, 21

    AASCU position, 20

    BEOGs, 51, 72–74

    government regulation, 51–53

    middle income students, 70–71

    origins, 30

    political factors, 24–25

    problems of distribution, 53–56

    public/private differences, 53, 72–73, 88

    Reagan Administration cuts, 81–82

    undergraduate scholarships, 37, 38

    versus institutional aid, 50–52

Student organizations, 13

"Subgovernments," 25

Sullivan (Richard H.), 45

Sullivan Report, 43–46

Supplemental Educational Opportunity Grants, 73

T

Tax credits, 19, 70

Teacher Corps, 38

Technical training: AACJC support, 22
Title IV, 46
Trends for future, 88–90
Truman (David), 66
"Tuesday Luncheon Club," 39, 86
Tuition
        AACJC position, 21
        AASCU position, 20
        public-private differential, 53
Typology of associations, 13–15

U
Umbrella organizations, 14, 15, 17, 65–66
Undergraduate degrees: from AASCU institutions, 20
University of Michigan, 76
Urban institutions, 18

V
Vietnam War, 43
Vocational education: AACJC support, 22
Voluntary associations: definitions and membership, 1–3

W
Washington, D.C.: association headquarters, 5
Washington Higher Education Secretariat (see American Council
    on Education/Secretariat)
Washington Post, 70, 80
Wilson (Logan), 17, 57, 58

ASHE-ERIC HIGHER EDUCATION REPORTS

Starting in 1983, the Association for the Study of Higher Education assumed cosponsorship of the Higher Education Reports with the ERIC Clearinghouse on Higher Education. For the previous 11 years, ERIC and the American Association for Higher Education prepared and published the reports.

Each report is the definitive analysis of a tough higher education problem, based on a thorough research of pertinent literature and institutional experiences. Report topics, identified by a national survey, are written by noted practitioners and scholars with prepublication manuscript reviews by experts.

Eight monographs (10 monographs before 1985) in the ASHE-ERIC Higher Education Report series are published each year, available individually or by subscription. Subscription to eight issues is $55 regular; $40 for members of AERA, AAHE and AIR: $35 for members of ASHE. (Add $7.50 outside the United States.)

Prices for single copies, including 4th class postage and handling, are $7.50 regular and $6.00 for members of AERA, AAHE, AIR, and ASHE ($6.50 regular and $5.00 for members for reports published before 1983). If faster 1st class postage is desired for U.S. and Canadian orders, add $.75 for each publication ordered: overseas, add $4.50. For VISA and MasterCard payments, include card number, expiration date, and signature. Orders under $25 must be prepaid. Bulk discounts are available on orders of 15 or more reports (not applicable to subscriptions). Order from the Publications Department. Association for the Study of Higher Education. One Dupont Circle. Suite 630, Washington, D.C. 20036, (202) 296-2597. Write for a publication list of all Higher Education Reports still available.

1985 Higher Education Reports now available

1. Flexibility in Academic Staffing: Effective Policies and Practices
   Kenneth P. Mortimer, Marque Bagshaw, and Andrew T. Masland

2. Associations in Action: The Washington, D.C., Higher Education Community
   Harland G. Bloland

1984 Higher Education Reports

1. Adult Learning: State Policies and Institutional Practices
   K. Patricia Cross and Anne-Marie McCartan

2. Student Stress: Effects and Solutions
   Neal A. Whitman, David C. Spendlove, and Claire H. Clark

3. Part-time Faculty: Higher Education at a Crossroads
   Judith M. Gappa

4. Sex Discrimination Law in Higher Education: The Lessons of the Past Decade
   J. Ralph Lindgren, Patti T. Ota, Perry A. Zirkel, and Nan Van Gieson

5. Faculty Freedoms and Institutional Accountability: Interactions and Conflicts
   Steven G. Olswang and Barbara A. Lee

6. The High-Technology Connection: Academic Industrial Cooperation for Economic Growth
   Lynn G. Johnson

7. Employee Educational Programs: Implications for Industry and Higher Education
   Suzanne W. Morse

8. Academic Libraries: The Changing Knowledge Centers of Colleges and Universities
   Barbara B. Moran

9. Futures Research and the Strategic Planning Process: Implications for Higher Education
   James L. Morrison, William L. Renfro, and Wayne I. Boucher

10. Faculty Workload: Research, Theory, and Interpretation
    Harold E. Yuker

1983 Higher Education Reports

1. The Path to Excellence: Quality Assurance in Higher Education
   Laurence R. Marcus, Anita O. Leone, and Edward D. Goldberg

2. Faculty Recruitment, Retention, and Fair Employment: Obligations and Opportunities
   John S. Waggaman

3. Meeting the Challenges: Developing Faculty Careers
   Michael C. T. Brookes and Katherine L. German

4. Raising Academic Standards: A Guide to Learning Improvement
   Ruth Talbott Keimig

5. Serving Learners at a Distance: A Guide to Program Practices
   Charles E. Feasley

6. Competence, Admissions, and Articulation: Returning to the Basics in Higher Education
   Jean L. Preer

7. Public Service in Higher Education: Practices and Priorities
   Patricia H. Crosson

8. Academic Employment and Retrenchment: Judicial Review and Administrative Action
   Robert M. Hendrickson and Barbara A. Lee

9. Burnout: The New Academic Disease
   Winifred Albizu Meléndez and Rafael M. de Guzmán

10. Academic Workplace: New Demands, Heightened Tensions
    Ann E. Austin and Zelda F. Gamson

Yes, I want to receive the other 7 reports in the 1985 ASHE-ERIC Higher Education Report series at the special discount price. I have just bought Report No. ____ at $7.50. Please deduct this amount from the price of my subscription.

"... A valuable series, especially for reviewing and revising academic programs. These reports can save us all from pitfalls and frustrations."

Mark H. Curtis, former President
Association of American Colleges

Dear Librarian,

I have just finished reading one of the 1985 ASHE-ERIC Higher Education Reports (ISSN 0884-0040). I found it outstanding and strongly recommend that our institution subscribe to the series. At $55.00 for 8 issues, it is a bargain.

Signed,

Name _____

Title _____

ASHE ERIC®

Association for the Study of Higher Education
The George Washington University
One Dupont Circle, Suite 630, Dept. 51
Washington, D.C. 20036
Phone: (202) 296-2597